Communication and Society
Editor: Jeremy Tunstall

The making of a television series

d

In the same series:

Journalists at work
J. Tunstall

PHILIP ELLIOTT

The making of a television series

a case study in the sociology of culture

Communication Arts Books
Hastings House, Publishers   New York 10016

Printed in Great Britain

In memory of
Roger Brown

Contents

Acknowledgements

This book and the study on which it is based was only made possible by the efforts of many people. As I have followed the convention of presenting the study without naming those involved, it is impossible to thank most of these people personally. Only the names of the various guests who appeared in the television series have been retained in the text, as they are already in the public domain. So too are the programmes themselves. This doubtless means that there will be those who will recognize who was involved in the production of the series and who will realize to whom this study is especially indebted. Job titles may lack the warmth of individual names, but there is no concealing the gratitude which is owing to the producer and the other members of the production team, to others in television who were connected with the production of this series and to those within Associated Television who helped to get the series and the research under way. In this connection special debt is owing to the executive producer and at an earlier stage the educational executive producer.

James D. Halloran played a crucial part in getting the project started. I am greatly indebted to him for preparing the way for the project and for establishing a setting in which a study of this type could take place at the Centre for Mass Communication Research. Professor Halloran has pressed for more attention in mass communication research to be given to the study of media organization, personnel and production processes. This project is a direct result.

I am also grateful to my colleagues at the Centre, all of whom have been a great help with discussion, comment and criticism. At an early stage, Dave Chaney and I worked together on the theoretical basis of the project and I am indebted to him for this collaboration and for subsequent discussions. I am also indebted to Jeremy Tunstall for making many useful comments.

The study of audience reactions to the series was carried out by Roger L. Brown who died in the spring of 1971. It is tragic that he will not see the work in its final form. I am deeply grateful to him for his collaboration.

For the audience study I wish to thank the three headmasters of the schools from which the adolescent sample was drawn and to the staff of the National College for the Training of Youth Leaders, of Vaughan College, University of Leicester, and of RAF Cranwell, in particular to Jim Corben, Terry Willits, Denis Rice and Squadron Leader John Towey. I am also grateful to the respondents themselves for returning between them more than one thousand questionnaires.

Charles Husband and Peggy Gray carried out calculations and analyses for both parts of the study. The study involved the secretarial staff at the Centre in a great deal of work which they have carried out with commendable fortitude; special thanks are due to Enid Nightingale, Winifred Jefferson, Florence Robinson and Anna Howse for typing the final version.

PHILIP ELLIOTT
Centre for Mass Communication Research,
University of Leicester,
August 1971

Introduction

The first formal step towards the setting up of the study reported in this book was taken in June 1965 when the then Head of Educational Broadcasting at ATV wrote to me, as Secretary of the Television Research Committee, asking for help with regard to 'audience research in connection with adult education programmes on television'. However, to provide a full account of how work came to be done we need to go back to the establishment of the Television Research Committee by the Home Secretary in 1963, or perhaps more specifically to the publication of the Committee's first Working Paper in 1964.*

In brief, the Committee's remit was to initiate and coordinate research into the influence of television and the other media on the perceptual processes, social attitudes and moral concepts of young people. The Committee and the financial support provided by ITA were direct products of public concern about alleged effects of television. This is by no means an unusual beginning for research in the social sciences, but what perhaps is unusual is that this Committee did not take the problem as given, i.e. as officially defined, but worked out its own interpretation of the terms of reference.

Conscious of the narrowness, the imbalance, the theoretical paucity and the service or administrative orientation of so much mass communication research in the past, the Committee used its unusual opportunity to attempt to revitalize the whole field

* *The Effects of Mass Communication – with Special Reference to Television*, Leicester University Press, 1964.

and to present an overall strategy.* Consequently, it was able to address itself to the questions more directly associated with the expressions of social concern referred to earlier, whilst at the same time it could stress the need to study the communication process not as a series of isolated relationships but within its full social context and as an integral part of the social system. By 1965, the Committee had formulated a policy, later adopted by the Centre, in which 'studies of the production process' were an integral part. In view of the nature of their earlier request, it is most encouraging to note that ATV accepted the research design presented to them, and which Philip Elliott was then able to develop and carry out when he started to work on the project in March 1967.

It would not be appropriate to deal with the question of the researcher/broadcaster relationship in full in an introductory statement, but some aspects of it are at least worth a mention. When ATV's Head of Educational Broadcasting approached the Television Research Committee on behalf of the ATV Education Advisory Committee, he was looking for information about the audience (actual and potential) for educational television programmes. It is not surprising that those responsible for programmes should turn to research for this sort of information (even though in this case the terms of reference and the publications of the Television Research Committee had a different emphasis) for, in general this is what they expect and what they have been led to expect from research.

Research which provides information about the size, composition and reactions of audiences, about the effectiveness of the message, and about the attractiveness or influence of certain forms of presentation – in short, research which serves the interests of the media as defined by those working in the media – is the research, sometimes the only research, favoured by the broadcaster. There are many reasons, some obvious, some not so obvious, why most broadcasters tend to prefer this sort of

* See *Problems of Television Research* (*A Progress Report of the Television Research Committee*), Leicester University Press, 1966.

research to studies which set out to examine the production process, decision-making, or the control, support and organization of broadcasting institutions.

Still, it would be unfair and misleading for us at Leicester to be over-critical on this score. The cool official reactions by the media in this country to the recommendations of the Television Research Committee in 1969 are, up to a point, offset by many examples of individual cooperation.

In acknowledging this valuable help, it is also recognized that there are understandable reasons why many other broadcasters are less happy about cooperating in the type of research referred to in these pages. I feel that one of our tasks is to help them to change their minds – as it is also our task to persuade the media research councils, trusts and other funding bodies to change their policies so that long-term, systematic research planning would become possible. Without this, the necessary broadening and deepening of our understanding of these vital social processes and institutions are not likely to be achieved.

It is hoped that the research diligently and imaginatively carried out and presented in this book by Philip Elliott will be an important step towards this objective.

PROFESSOR JAMES D. HALLORAN

1

A case study of television production

Television, the most recent of the mass media, already has a dominant place in the national culture. The medium has had an impact on most forms of art and entertainment. Most people have accepted a substantial period of viewing as a permanent part of their lives. Many have asked questions about the effect of this new medium on other people usually on those inferior in age or social status. Concern with television as a potentially corrupting or disruptive influence has sprung, at least in part, from an acquaintance with its content. But there have been few attempts to investigate the genesis of this content. A few ill-defined and largely uninvestigated suppositions have been exchanged in popular debate: suppositions about the consequences of commercialism and large scale organizations for creative work, about possible links between the media and other centres of power in society and about the distinctive life style and philosophy to be found among those working in television and the other media. There has also been little academic debate about production for the mass media, either within the sociologies of art and culture or within the field of mass communication research. Even when such academic debate has taken place, popular supposition has often been a more important ingredient than disciplined research.

This book is based on a study of the production of a seven programme documentary series, *The Nature of Prejudice*, made in the autumn of 1967 for Associated Television (ATV) and transmitted over most of the Independent Television Network in the spring of 1968. The production study was coupled with

an exploratory audience research project (reported in Chapter
6) and with specific analyses of programme content. This provides a unique case study of the communication process in the
round.[1] As more and more people look to television for information and entertainment, it becomes increasingly important
to ask not only what effect does it have on them, what do they
make of it, what do they get out of it; but also how is it that
these are the programmes made available, how is the material
selected and created, how do the television organizations and
the 'new priesthood' working within them perform their
functions, indeed how do they see their function and does their
view agree with that of their audience? To translate these
questions into sociological terms, the central aim of this book
is to throw light on the relationship between culture and social
structure as it is mediated through television.

This may seem a grandiose claim for a monograph based on
a case study of one television series. Although the data available
from the study refer to one particular and no doubt individual
case, it can be used to illuminate general features of the television production situation and to explore the relationship
between society, producers and audience. A case study approach
is not the only way of tackling this problem, just as participant
observation is not the only possible method:* it is to be hoped
that this research will be a prelude to further study of the same
problems using a wider range of methods. Nevertheless, at this
stage in the development of media sociology, advantages can be
claimed for this particular approach and method.

At a practical level one way to gain access to the research
situation is through the support and cooperation of particular
individuals. This method matches the personal, particularistic
features of media organizations and their occupational milieu.
General, formal approaches may be met with suspicious re-
sistance, similar to that shown by members of other organizations and occupational groups, but compounded by such

---

* See Appendix B for a discussion of the method of participant observation
as used in this study.

factors as the publicity associated with work for the media and, internally, by the nature of career routes and employment opportunities. In this case two executive producers were crucial at different stages in keeping the idea for the series alive within the company and ensuring that when it was eventually brought to fruition, the research plans were also realized. For two years prior to the production team starting work on *The Nature of Prejudice*, plans had been laid by the first executive producer for a thirteen programme, adult education series. The second executive producer, taking over these plans on the departure of his colleague, changed the series to one of seven ordinary documentaries, a type of programme more in line with his own interests and responsibilities. Like any other programme series *The Nature of Prejudice* had its own peculiar pre-history, circumscribed by the organizational framework within which it developed and by the personnel who handled it. There is a sense in which it was both 'unique' and 'typical', but no sense in which it was a 'put up job', a series arranged for the benefit of the research study.

One drawback to participant observation as a method of research is that the situation observed and the account recorded may have been arranged for the benefit of the researcher. A good answer to this criticism is that deliberate distortion is much less likely to occur if an observer is present over a period of time, than it is, for example, in responses to a questionnaire or interview. Moreover, other goals, such as getting the work done or the programmes produced, inevitably take precedence over any aim to mislead the researcher. Participant observation is not so much a single method as a battery of methods, including most of the other research techniques in embryo. For this reason it was particularly suited to the present project, enabling a wide range of research questions and interests to be handled continuously. A specific technique would have required an initial decision on the precise focus of the research. This is not to say that the research had no focus at the start, but rather from the outset that there was a continual interaction between theoretical assumptions and interests, general and specific hypotheses and the data of the particular case. This case study approach, like the 'extended case' method in social anthropology, on which it is to some extent modelled,[2] incorporates the dynamics of behaviour and process while allowing beliefs and organization to be explored in more static, structural terms.

At a theoretical level another reason for adopting this particular approach to the study was that it directed attention towards the process through which cultural artefacts are produced. The research was based on the premise that there is a relationship between artistic and cultural forms and social structure and process.

The case study approach assumed that one way to identify and analyse this relationship was by examining the actual process of artistic and cultural creation. There has been considerable dispute within the sociology of art about the nature of the relationship, but there have been surprisingly few attempts to investigate it directly in the process and organization of artistic and cultural production.[3] Such attempts have been inhibited by beliefs about the importance of the individual in the process of artistic creation. The idea of the artist as an individual creator has gained currency through romantic reinterpretation of the Renaissance and became the basis of a creative artistic ideology during the nineteenth century. The ideology has been particularly important in directing sociologists away from what appeared to be an individual phenomenon. For example Goldmann, writing of the approach adopted by himself and other followers of Lukacs has commented 'at bottom we probably thought that richness (in a work of art) attached itself primarily to the individuality of the writer and could not be approached from a sociological perspective'.[4] Similarly, Huaco in a study of film art rejects the possibility of studying individual film-makers and instead concentrates on identifiable schools or waves, even though he starts from a straight superstructure/base model.[5]

The self-denying ordinance which has kept sociologists from

studying the artist, has led instead to a concentration on the artistic output. One result has been large scale equations of the relationship between art and society such as Dewey's claim that art is a manifestation of 'the collective spirit of an age'.[6] Simplification and generalization are inherent in this approach of examining artistic content for its social meaning. They are necessary to fit art or society into the two halves of the equation. Sorokin's theory of ideational and sensate cultures illustrates this type of work at an extreme level of socio-historical generalization.[7] Middle range theories have varied from the relatively weak proposition that art in some way reflects society to stronger assertions that art restrains or encourages social change.[8] *Post hoc* analysis of content may provide plausible evidence for any of these propositions; but criteria for deciding between them are lacking without a detailed examination of the genesis of cultural output and of its reception by the audience and by society.

By concentrating on the content sociologists and literary critics have been able to point to relationships between the artist's work and the society in which they were created, which were probably not apparent to the artist himself. This has reinforced the argument against studying the individual artist in his social setting. For example, Lowenthal has pointed out that because 'Creative literature conveys many levels of meaning, some intended by the author, some quite unintentional ... It is the task of the sociologist of literature to relate the experience of the writer's imaginary characters and situations to the historical climate from which they derive'.[9] Individual creative genius is one explanation of the process of cultural osmosis through which the writer or artist acts as the unwitting interpreter of his time.

Post hoc analysis of content appears to enjoy at least one advantage over the production case study approach, adopted in this book. It appears to bring the analyst closer to the whole, to generalizations about socio-cultural periods and systems, rather than leaving him to deal with the parts which, even in com-

bination, may turn out to be less than the whole.[10] But this is
not a difference inherent in the two approaches so much as in
the traditional styles of work which are associated with them.
Studying the production process does not mean simply examining consciously articulated production intentions, nor simply
treating technological and organizational systems as deter-
minants and constraints on a creative process. These can be
studied, but within the broader aim of comprehending the
production situation, the occupational cultures which develop
within it, and investigating the way these articulate with wider
cultural systems based on the social positions of different groups
and the conflicts of interest between them. A phenomenological
approach to social research, keeping in sight the dialectic between idea and reality and the over-arching social importance
of abstract institutions and groups seems to offer a way of
approaching 'socio-cultural wholes' from the bottom up.[11]
Without the support of further comparative work, data from
the present study cannot carry us far towards an analysis of
socio-cultural wholes, but the final chapter of this book makes
a start in that direction, one which could be extended further
by using the same approach.

Direct study of the artist's position in the social structure and
of the creative process itself is more attractive in the case of the
mass media than when dealing with an isolated individual
creator, working through a traditional art form. Large scale
production organizations, par excellence Hollywood in the
heyday of the studio system, have appeared to involve some of
the specialization, division of labour and standardization of
product that is associated with mass production systems in
other types of industry. Coser, in his survey of intellectual roles
in modern society, has accepted the equation between mass
media producers and other types of mass production worker,
arguing that they no longer have individual creative responsibility but contribute to a rationalized, specialized process,
which alienates them in the same way as other workers.[12]

More specific analysis of the production systems within media organizations might suggest some qualifications to this equation.[13] In terms of Woodward's typology of organization systems the unit or small batch output of media organisations is not sufficiently large, or standard, to allow complete rationalization of the production system.[14] Each film or episode in a television series has to be a unique product however closely it may approximate to others in a similar genre. A continuous tension develops between individuation and standardization in production for the media. Moreover artists and producers are able to pursue careers in contexts wider than a single organization. Cultural production offers a wider range of rewards in terms of career, status and intrinsic satisfaction than are available in an industrial job.

One powerful impulse towards standardization of output within media organizations is the need to satisfy an audience with a commercially marketable product. The strength of this impulse has varied from medium to medium. Elements in the 'mass continuum' postulated by McQuail, such as increasing audience size and heterogeneity, support a process of standardization.[15] Others, such as the tendency for a complete service to replace smaller units of output, have at least made countervailing tendencies possible.

The commercial basis of the media and their economic dependence on a large audience market has also contributed to the suspicion with which their creative and cultural function has been regarded. Commercial and administrative goals appear to conflict with an artistic and creative system of values. This assertion of a separate creative value system has provided a basis for the development of a separate professional ideology among those working at production level within media organizations.[16] It provides a theoretical justification for professional independence within the work organizations and appeals to values which are shared by others in the society. Raymond Williams, for example, concludes his account of the development of commercial media in modern society with a plea for a structure which would encourage greater professional freedom and so remedy the defects which he detects in the current commercial system.[17]

This professional ideology can also be used to combat the attacks on media output as 'low culture', levelled by those concerned with a debasement of the traditional 'high culture'.[18] Individual creativity is itself part of the value system of 'high culture'. The mass media, especially the visual media of cinema and television, have widely disseminated different types of content derived from both 'high' and 'low' cultural forms. The mass media seem to threaten class divisions in both cultural consumption and cultural creation. Most discussion of the role of the artist in the media has been couched, at least implicitly, in high cultural terms, but Hall and Whanel have shown how urban working-class folk culture has been subject to a similar process of change. They trace the gradual separation of audience and performer roles within the folk culture, a separation which was begun by the establishment of the music halls and which reached its epitome in the star system of the cinema; but parallel to this development they also trace a tendency towards standardization of the cultural output. They seek to draw a distinction between 'popular culture', relevant to the life styles and life experiences of the audience, and 'mass culture', which in another sense is separated from the audience, playing upon their feelings and emotions by using standard, established techniques.

This brief discussion of critiques of cultural production in the mass media shows the wider issues about the relationship between cultural production and social structure which this study will raise. In the final chapter we shall return to the points made by friends and critics of the media alike when we endeavour to derive a more general theory of mass communication and media production from the particular data of the case study.

Anyone who expects mass communication research to provide another source of guidance towards theoretical formulations of the problem is doomed to disappointment. For reasons which lie in the history and structure of mass communication research itself studies of the communicator and of the organization of media production have been slow to develop.[19] For similar reasons, hidden assumptions and easy analogies have taken the place of theoretical analysis of the communication process. Recently, however, there have been signs of a shift of interest. In Britain, the Television Research Committee has consistently advocated that studies of the audience should be set within the wider context of the media as social institutions.[20] Several recent surveys of the field have suggested that more attention should be given to studies of media organizations, personnel and production processes; and some research, notably by Burns and Blumler, has appeared.[21]

One latent consequence of the preoccupation with audience effect in mass communication research has been the acceptance of an implicit model of communication in which the communicator is the source of such influence and effect. Study of persuasive communications – wartime propaganda, advertising, even anti-prejudice propaganda – fostered the idea of the persuasive communicator.[22] In Lasswell's famous paradigm the 'who' is presumed to be saying something to somebody with some purpose.[23]

As McQuail has pointed out, 'mass communications has not prospered under the shadow of mass society theory'.[24] There is considerable confusion between its various versions, but they share in common the lack of any empirical base. Mass society theory tends to credit the media with important functions of persuasion, control and manipulation. Wright Mills, for example, was prepared to argue that in the media, 'entire brackets of professions and industries are in the "opinion business" impersonally manipulating the public for hire',[25] while Marcuse has suggested a less direct process in which the media create and manipulate false needs.[26] In the first case 'at the end of the road there is totalitarianism', in the second, totalitarianism is already here in the shape of 'a comfortable, smooth, reasonable democratic unfreedom'. Marcuse is prepared to argue that 'the non-functioning of television and the allied media might thus begin to achieve what the inherent contradictions of capitalism did not achieve – the disintegration of the system. The creation of repressive needs has long since become part of socially necessary labour – necessary in the sense that without it, the established mode of production could not be maintained.'

Other theorists have developed a similar argument that the media are in a general sense system maintaining, but from the very different perspective of functionalism.[27] Where the mass society theorist tends to see an economic or political conspiracy, the functionalist tends to see the needs of the social system. Accordingly he evaluates the media's function positively rather than negatively. McCormack, for example, argues that the media's function is to provide segmentalized, urbanized mass society with an integrating gestalt:[28] 'The supreme test of the mass media is not whether it meets the criteria of art or the criteria of knowledge, but how well it provides an integration of experience.' Some studies of developing countries have credited the media with a similar importance in providing the integration necessary to encourage industrialization and social change.[29] 'Nation-building' suggests the development of a common consciousness, but a more important part of the process could well be expressed in Marcusian terms, the creation of false needs.

A second model of the communication process has developed as a latent consequence of an easy analogy with interpersonal communication. Communication through the media, so the argument runs, is a disjointed and imperfect form of ordinary, human two-person communication. In human communication multiple verbal and visual channels are available for communication and feed-back. The mass media separate communicator and audience, making feed-back tenuous. It is especially difficult for the communicator to pitch his message at a level at which it will appeal to, or be understood by a heterogeneous, mass audience. Interpersonal communication becomes an unattainable ideal to which media systems aspire. De Fleur, among others, has asserted there are no fundamental differences between mass communication and simpler forms of interpersonal communication, an assertion which looks insecure resting simply on the analogy.[30]

The bulk of the empirical research so far conducted on the role of the mass communicator has been carried out on newsmen and newsmaking for press or television. This has led to a third model of mass communication, as a process of information flow. Although the 'gatekeepers' who stand astride these channels of flow have sometimes been considered as candidates for the position of 'who' in the Lasswellian paradigm, one of the important differences between the 'flow' model of communication and the 'persuasive' and 'interpersonal' models already discussed is that it does not need to assume that the process was initiated by an active communicator.[31] This point has been brought out by the distinction Westley and Maclean make in their conceptual model for communication research between 'purposive' and 'non-purposive' communicators.[32] Their distinction which relies on identifying the intentions of the communicator-audience relationship from that inherent in the persuasive model. Instead of stressing the way the media act upon society and their audience, Westley and Maclean point to a reciprocal relationship between the growth of audience needs and the development of communication channels to service those needs. Communication media are introduced when non-purposive communicators recognize that particular groups within the general population have special needs based on common problems, circumstances or interests which can be served by a communication channel. This model takes the commercial structure of the media for granted. The 'non-purposive' communicator recognizing audience needs is more familiar as the seller in the free market economy, only this time he is in the business of marketing 'special symbol systems'. On the face of it, it seems unlikely that anyone could confuse the communication industry with a perfect market.

The latent importance of commercial considerations is highlighted in the Westley and Maclean model by the use of the concept 'satisfaction' to link media and audience. Whereas the persuasive model suggested questions about the effectiveness of communication in persuading, influencing, even entertaining the audience, the Westley and Maclean model suggests that the media should try to maximize audience satisfaction. In a later paper Maclean shows that he has no doubts of the implications which this approach has for mass communication research:[33] 'My general question is: What kind of "Audience" research fed to key mass communicators in what form can best help them to create products more satisfying to their customers?'

Satisfaction has replaced *communication* as the link between media and audience. The contrast between these two relationships is similar to the contrast between 'popular culture' and 'mass culture' made by Hall and Whanel and noted above. It is also similar to the contrast which Raymond Williams has made between commercial popular newspapers and an earlier tradition of radical journalism.[34] Williams has suggested that modern commercial media are unlikely to develop a relationship with their audience based on communication and response, such as that enjoyed by nineteenth-century political journalists and pamphleteers. 'In the main, the difference of style is clear: the radical style is one of genuine arousal: the commercial style is one of apparent arousal as a cover for an eventual, if temporary, satisfaction'. The type of mass communication research which seeks to provide the conditions for apparent arousal invites an even more swingeing critique.

A theoretical framework was formulated at the start of the present study drawing on work in the sociology of art and culture, industrial and organizational sociology and mass communication research, some of which has been discussed above.[35] The aim of the framework was to show how the projected case study could deal with both the statics and dynamics of cultural production by looking at programme-making as a social process, and by setting the programme-makers into a series of socio-cultural contexts: the work group, the organization, the medium or occupational milieu and the general socio-cultural system.

Intensive field work for the study lasted just over four months, from the time the production team first assembled, until the studio recording of the seventh programme. Data collection and the daily process of ordering and summarizing the data to develop and test out generalizations, were guided by the initial theoretical framework. But this study, in common with others,[36] soon developed its own momentum and, in later chapters, we shall show how data from the study altered and sharpened many of the initial questions and assumptions reviewed in this chapter.

In the course of this book we shall examine production for television as part of a relay system through which the society as audience is presented with an image of itself, the society as source. This research strategy is focused upon the role of the professional communicator as the creator of the intervening image – a different model of the mass communication process from the three discussed above.[37]

Three sets of factors define the situation within which the professional communicator works: the society as source: the society as audience; and the impact of the technical, organizational and occupational structure in which the communicator finds himself in the course of the production process itself. The study reported in later chapters is focused on the activities of production personnel and on the process of programme production itself. Technical, organizational and economic factors were not tackled directly, only in so far as they impinged upon the production process. In Chapter 7 an attempt is made to delineate some of the salient features of television organization; that account is also focused on the 'shop floor' level. A broader study of media economics and organization is long overdue but is not attempted here.

In the final chapter the scope of the analysis is widened to draw out the implications of the case study for a discussion of television and communication in society, elaborating the issues raised in this chapter about the relationship between the media, their cultural output and the society in which they operate. In this chapter we have discussed these issues in terms of both the sociology of culture and mass communication research; whereas the former has been mainly concerned with fictional cultural output, the latter has been mainly concerned with non-fictional output, as is the present study. It may be objected to the attempt to integrate these two approaches, on the grounds that documentary production does not involve artistic creativity and is, therefore, qualitatively different from the art and literature which has been the traditional concern of the sociology of art. The final chapter takes up the similarities and differences between documentary production and other types of production for television. The aim will be to erect a typology of the mass communication process to be developed by future research, in particular by the study of fictional programme production. For undoubtedly, there is a great need for a fuller understanding of the way in which the media organizations and the personnel who operate them, fill their central position in the culture of modern society.

REFERENCES

1. The closest parallels are journalistic accounts of media production, such as Lillian Ross on the making of the feature film *The Red Badge of Courage – Picture* (London: Gollancz) 1953; or autobiographical accounts, such as M. Miller and E. Rhodes, *Only You Dick Daring* (New York: Wm. Sloane Assocs.) 1964, on the trials and tribulations of a television writer on an adventure series in America.

2. See in particular Max Gluckman's introduction and the paper by J. Van Velsen, 'The Extended Case Method and Situational Analysis' in A. L. Epstein (ed.) *The Craft of Social Anthropology* (London: Tavistock) 1967.

3. For some exceptions see however I. Watt, *The Rise of the Novel* (Harmondsworth: Penguin) 1953; J. H. Mueller, *The American Symphony Orchestra: A Social History of Musical Taste* (Bloomington, Indiana: Indiana University Press) 1951.

4. L. Goldmann, 'Criticism and Dogmatism in Literature' in D.

Cooper (ed.) *The Dialectics of Liberation* (Harmondsworth: Penguin) 1968, p. 144.

5. G. Huaco, *The Sociology of Film Art* (New York: Basic Books) 1965.

6. J. Dewey, *Art as Experience* (New York: G. P. Putnam's Sons) 1934.

7. P. Sorokin, *Social and Cultural Dynamics, Vol. 1, Fluctuations of Forms of Art* (Cincinnati: American Book Co.) 1937.

8. A summary of the field stressing these different approaches may be found in M. C. Albrecht, 'The Relationship of Literature and Society', *American Journal of Sociology*, 59, 1954, pp. 425–436.

9. L. Lowenthal, *Literature and the Image of Man* (Boston: The Beacon Press) 1953.

10. Goldmann has attacked the approach of relating manifest content to manifest features of the social structure on this ground. The following remarks are intended as an answer to an extension of Goldmann's argument. In essence the point is if 'structure' can be studied through the work set in its social context, it can also be approached through the study of cultural production in its social context. See L. Goldmann, 'The Sociology of Literature: Status and Problems of Method', *International Social Science Journal*, 19, 1967; also *The Hidden God* (trans. P. Thody) (London: Routledge) 1964 and for a recent English commentary on Goldmann's work, Raymond Williams, 'Literature and Sociology', *New Left Review*, 67, 1971.

11. See in particular P. Berger and T. Luckman, *The Social Construction of Reality* (London: Allen Lane) 1967 and some of the papers in D. Emmet and A. MacIntyre, *Sociological Theory and Philosophical Analysis* (London: Macmillan) 1970.

12. L. Coser, *Men of Ideas* (New York: Free Press) 1965. This point of view is derived especially from the situation of the movie script writers who compared their situation unfavourably with the traditional, independent novelist. On Hollywood see also H. Powdermaker, *Hollywood: The Dream Factory* (New York: Little Brown) 1951; L. Boston, *Hollywood* (New York: Harcourt Brace) 1941.

13. See R. Blauner, *Alienation and Freedom* (Chicago: Chicago University Press) 1964, for a comparative study of alienation in different types of production situation.

14. J. Woodward, *Management and Technology* (London: HMSO) 1958.

15. D. McQuail, *Towards a Sociology of Mass Communications* (London: Collier-Macmillan) 1969.

16. As exemplified by current attempts at occupational organization within television and the press.

17. R. Williams, *Communications* (Rev. ed.) (Harmondsworth: Penguin) 1968; *The Long Revolution* (London: Chatto & Windus) 1961.

18. For a summary and important discussion of these arguments see S. Hall and P. Whanel, *The Popular Arts* (London: Hutchinson) 1964.

19. See R. L. Brown, 'Approaches to the Historical Development of Mass Media Studies' in J. Tunstall (ed.) *Media Sociology* (London: Constable) 1970.

20. The Television Research Committee, *Problems of Television Research, Progress Report No. 1* (Leicester: Leicester University Press; 1966; *Second Progress Report and Recommendations* (Leicester: Leicester University Press) 1969.

21. J. D. Halloran, *The Effects of Mass Communication: with special reference to television* (Leicester: Leicester University Press) 1965; D. McQuail *op. cit.*; J. Tunstall, introduction to *Media Sociology op. cit.*, a volume which also includes papers by Tom Burns and Jay Blumler.

22. E. Katz, 'Communication Research and The Image of Society', *American Journal of Sociology* 65, 1959, pp. 435–440.

23. H. Lasswell, 'The Structure and Function of Communication in Society' in L. Bryson (ed.) *The Communication of Ideas* (New York) 1948.

24. D. McQuail, *op. cit.*

25. C. Wright Mills, *The Power Elite* (New York: Oxford University Press) 1959.

26. H. Marcuse, *One Dimensional Man* (London: Sphere Books edn.) 1968.

27. See for example M. de Fleur, *Theories of Mass Communication* (New York: McKay) 1966.

28. T. McCormack, 'Social Theory and the Mass Media', *Canadian Review of Economic and Political Science*, 27, 1961, pp. 479–489. Quotation from p. 488.

29. As for example in L. W. Pye (ed.) *Communication and Political Development* (Princeton: Princeton University Press) 1963.

30. M. De Fleur, *op. cit.*

31. The classic 'gatekeeper' study, much replicated, is D. M. White, 'The Gatekeeper: A Case Study in the Selection of News', *Journalism Quarterly*, 27, 1950, pp. 383–390.

32. B. H. Westley and M. S. Maclean, jnr., 'A Conceptual Model for Communication Research', *Journalism Quarterly*, 34, 1957, pp. 31–38.

33. M. S. Maclean, jnr., 'Systems of News Communication' in L. Thayer (ed.) *Communication: Theory and Research* (Springfield, Illinois: C. Thomas) 1967.

34. R. Williams in R. Boston (ed.) *The Press We Deserve* (London: Routledge) 1970. Quotation from p. 21.

35. P. Elliott and D. Chaney, 'A Sociological Framework for the Study of Television Production', *Sociological Review*, 17, 1969, pp. 355–375.

36. See for example Blanche Geer's account of 'First Days in the Field' in P. E. Hammond (ed.) *Sociologists at Work* (New York: Basic Books) 1964, ch. 11.

37. On the 'professional communicator' see J. Carey, 'The Communication Revolution and the Professional Communicator', *Sociological Review Monograph*, 13, 1969, pp. 23–28.

2

Starting work on the series

The Nature of Prejudice never got beyond the planning stage as an adult education series. Nevertheless there were indications that the production system for adult education programmes differed from the documentary production process through which the programmes were finally produced. There was greater specialization and routinization in the educational production system. An academic adviser was appointed to develop the idea for the series and write programme outlines. If the series had followed the normal procedure, these would then have been passed to a scriptwriter to write up as programmes. A director would then have worked from the scripts to make the programmes visual. At ATV at this time a single producer was responsible for most of the educational output. He specialized entirely in educational programmes and was quite capable of handling several series on quite diverse subjects at the same time. This was made possible by dividing up the process of production, so that many of the producer's functions could be delegated and his main task was coordination.

In abstract the educational production system can be conceived as a funnel, through which passes a body of knowledge coming from an expert adviser outside the medium. As it passes through, it is selected, shaped and processed by the production personnel to fit the medium of television, in particular, its visual potential. It was clear from exchanges between the adviser and the producer, working on *The Nature of Prejudice*, that the television personnel retained editorial control and that visual considerations played a large part in deciding how such control would be exercised.

No academic adviser was employed to work on the documentary series. This was not only a difference in production system: it also had an impact on the research. The original plan had been to carry out the study through the adviser as well as independent observation. Once the series had switched styles the research depended simply on independent observation and there was no other connection with the production team.

THE DOCUMENTARY PRODUCTION TEAM

Educational and general documentary programmes were both among the responsibilities of the Factual Programme Department within ATV. At the time work started on *The Nature of Prejudice* the main regular series in production in the department was *Good Evening*, a talking variety show introduced by Jonathan King. This ran against a similar programme on BBC built around Simon Dee. Prior to that the main series had been *On the Braden Beat*. Non-fictional programmes were not usually an important part of ATV's output, but they had acquired significance at this time as a source of prestige with the ITA. Company contracts were soon to be reallocated in the ITV network. The department functioned as a fairly self-contained unit under two associate heads, who supervised the work and took the executive responsibility. The fact that these two executives occupied almost parallel positions at the head of the department was a source of tension. Each appeared to be particularly concerned to keep an eye on what the other was doing. In terms used by Burns and Stalker, their parallel appointment showed the existence of a political system and status structure alongside the working organization of the company.*

The core production team for *The Nature of Prejudice* was

* Burns, T. and Stalker, G. M., *The Management of Innovation*, London, Tavistock, 1961.

B

made up of a producer, director, researcher, production assistant (p.a.) and, at later stages, a presenter. The *producer* contracted for the series by one of the two associate heads (subsequently referred to as the *executive producer*) had only recently completed two 'one-shot' documentaries for ATV. He and the executive producer had been contemporaries at an earlier date in the BBC. The producer had a considerable reputation from his past career in both BBC and ITV. He was one of those who had followed the well-trod path from wartime military intelligence, through the BBC Overseas Service, to the home department of the BBC. He had held executive positions in both the BBC and an independent company before deciding to take up programme production on a free-lance basis. He hoped that as a producer, rather than an executive, he would be able to realize his own ideas on the screen.

The *director* appointed to the series was also a free-lance, though he worked regularly for ATV on adult education programmes and documentaries. He had previously made documentary series for this same Sunday time-slot, working jointly as director and producer. He started his career in the film industry and then spent some time with Granada and with National Educational Television in the United States. His father was a public figure, well known for his television appearances.

The *researcher* was recommended to the producer by the executive producer for whom she had recently been working. After graduating from Oxford the researcher had worked for *Private Eye*, giving her a wide range of contacts in journalism. Although now a free-lance, she had been on the staff at ATV in the past. She was hoping to move to another production organization to work on programmes which were more 'socially significant' (in a general sense) than ATV's usual output. She was glad, however, to have the opportunity to work with someone of the producer's reputation. The p.a. joined the team later once work on the series had started.

THE AIM OF THE SERIES

Before production work started the producer outlined his general views on prejudice and sketched the aim of the series as he saw it. He defined prejudice as an attitude towards a distinct group of people or phenomena which is 'always irrational, deeply emotional and deeply held, impervious to argument or reason'. It had to be an attitude widely shared. The producer ruled out individual likes and dislikes. He felt that while there was a minority of very bigoted individuals with particular personality characteristics, social conditions played an important part in producing specific prejudices among the majority. For example, he suspected that British imperial history had played a large part in conditioning British attitudes towards coloured people. Similarly he felt outgroup hostility was likely to develop at the points of contact and competition between different groups. Apart from the problems of race and colour, he was particularly struck by the examples of religious prejudice current in Northern Ireland and Scotland. He suggested that these religious prejudices were gradually being eroded away, like the social prejudice between different classes which had been a feature of pre-war Britain. But now there were signs of a new prejudice developing, between different generations.

At a personal level the producer admitted that his strongest prejudice was against the attitude, common among the upper classes in Italy and to a lesser extent in Britain, that those beneath them in society were less than human and unworthy of notice. He also disliked authority in its bureaucratic, dehumanizing forms. For example, he saw the hospital queues of the National Health Service as a minor manifestation of essentially the same phenomena as the apartheid policies of South Africa. For the producer the whole problem of prejudice was closely bound up with this 'dehumanizing process' which he so intensely disliked. He had no doubt that prejudice was a bad thing and that attempts should be made to irradicate it.

Nevertheless, he was not going to attempt a frontal assault in the programmes. He saw his function as collecting 'evidence' from which 'conclusions' could be drawn in the programmes by himself, invited speakers and, by extension, the audience. He doubted whether the media could do much to combat prejudice unaided.

> Your media of communication I think probably can only present people with facts or with views which they may conceivably take and hold in their minds and be marginally affected by. But these things will only be effective when some other change is taking place. For instance . . . if a wave of intense racialism was sweeping the country, I don't think it could be stopped by the mass media.

The producer's views about prejudice were initially the most important source for ideas about subject areas to be covered in the programmes. The executive producer discussed his ideas for the series with the producer when he commissioned him to make the programmes. They agreed in general terms that the series should examine prejudice in all its aspects and not concentrate exclusively on race and colour. The extent to which executives detail their own ideas for a programme or require to see at least a rough synopsis before allowing production to proceed, seems to vary with the experience and reputation of the producer. In this case the producer did not receive any detailed instructions, simply a general outline of the plans for the series, and he was not required to prepare any synopses.

The producer hoped that further ideas for the programmes would develop within the production team once they started work. In particular he expected that the director, who came from a different social background – Eton and Oxford – might provide a foil to his own liberal inclinations.* In practice the director, together with most other television personnel, shared much the same liberal outlook. At the first meeting between the producer and the director, the main points of discussion were

---

* Liberal with a small 'l'.

possible subjects for the programmes.* These were secondarily related to the likely methods of presentation and budget costs. Five days later at a second meeting to work out detailed budget estimates, this relationship was reversed. The main topic then was methods of presentation into which possible subjects might be fitted. In this and the following chapter we shall discuss how programme ideas were generated through three chains of factors. The producer played the central part in one of these, the *subject chain*; the second, the *presentation chain*, was based on the budget allocated to the series and the modes of presentation it entailed; the third, the *contact chain*, centred on the range of contacts available to the production team.

THE SUBJECT CHAIN

Two types of programme ideas were mentioned in the first discussion between the producer and the director. First, general ideas of subject areas which 'ought to be covered' and second, specific ideas of particular items suitable for use in a programme. The broad subject areas reflected the producer's beliefs about the types of prejudice most salient in contemporary society, based on his reading and his own experience. The subject areas mentioned in this first meeting were (in the order they came up):

1 Racial and colour prejudice
2 Religious prejudice
3 Inter-generational prejudice
4 Inter-sexual prejudice
5 National prejudice between countries
6 Social prejudice
7 The wide variety of forms and expressions of prejudice
8 Prejudiced people and the victims of prejudice
9 The origins of prejudice

This list divides apparently fortuitously between the first six items, all specific types of prejudice, and the last three, more

* Strictly speaking this was not the first meeting. The producer had seen the director briefly on a previous occasion to explain the research attached to the series and to prepare him for the later presence of an observer.

general topics centred on the phenomenon of prejudice as a whole. At a later stage the producer abandoned completely the idea of having one programme to each specific type of prejudice.

These general subject areas were included within the producer's plans for approaching the series as a whole. This was focused on prejudice as a general and many-sided phenomenon. At the end of the meeting the producer summarized this aim:

> I think we should want to aim at presenting a variety of types of prejudice and prejudiced individuals so that at the end – if we go ahead with the idea of putting it all to a panel of experts to consider – then we can present, or get them to present, some generalizations about what prejudice is; whether there is such a fellow as a prejudiced individual and what makes him that way, so that they (the public) will get some understanding of the problem and what causes it.

All the specific ideas which were raised at this meeting for specific programme items can be related to at least one of the broad subject areas. All were suggested as possible illustrations of one of these general areas. Thus the subject chain provides one set of factors which account for the genesis of specific items in the programmes. This chain is shown in schematic form in Diagram I.

The presentation chain

The subject chain did not account completely and exhaustively for everything. The time-slot allocated to the programme, the budget available and customary methods of programme production were all closely interdependent. These factors lay behind the presentation chain which can be illustrated by the following exchange between the producer and the director in the first meeting.

Producer: Now looking ahead what we ought to do is concentrate all our filming in one period of time.
Director: Yes that would be nice.
Producer: Yes, this is the most economical way of doing it

DIAGRAM I

THE SUBJECT CHAIN

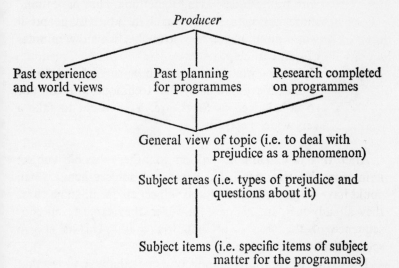

obviously. You book a crew for three, four days or whatever . . .

Director: I hope we can afford more than that . . .

Producer: . . . so that . . . well how much. A week?

Director: Well, I would normally reckon filming at £100 a day . . .

Producer: Yes . . .

Director: . . . and on that sort of budget I would certainly think we ought to be able to film, I would like to try and be able to film, two days a programme, or a day and a half a programme easily.

Producer: So that's two weeks.

Director: I'd like to be able to.

Producer: Well, we'll have to sit down and do some sums.

Director: Put it like this, if the subject was available without having to wait for it to bob up in front of a camera . . . It would be nice if we could get some fresh film in each programme to illustrate what we are talking about. If only of the sort of type like the Stork Margarine ads where people are right there saying it with traffic noise, saying something. They have found those enormously successful in advertising and it gets a point across very strongly. Just a few minutes of that can help.

Producer: Yes sure – what you've got to be sure of and do, of course, if you are using that technique, you can't be so unbalanced as Stork are. You've got to take a very wide spectrum . . .

After this discussion moved on to other possible subject items for film treatment. They were all subject items which could have originated through the subject chain. In some cases they already had. In this case, however, they came up in consequence of the second presentation chain. This is shown schematically in Diagram II.

The exchange from the first meeting quoted above shows that this chain depended at crucial points on the beliefs of the production personnel about modes of presentation suggested by different budgets and about appropriate uses for these different modes. Although the variety of specific modes available is very large, they can for present purposes be divided into two – film and studio.

For a number of reasons film is more highly valued by production personnel than studio modes of presentation. First, because of the way the programme budgets are drawn up, film is more expensive than studio production. Therefore, it is scarcer and its use marks out the programme and its producers from the usual run. In ATV the expense of film production was partly due to a budgetary device used to encourage full use of the company's large studio complex. Film costs appeared on the programme budget whereas most studio costs were hidden. This had another consequence that agreeing a budget included no guarantee that studio facilities would be available. Such facilities were controlled by executives at Elstree who could

DIAGRAM II

THE PRESENTATION CHAIN

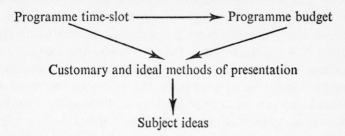

create problems for those belonging to opposing factions within the internal politics of the company by making studio facilities difficult for them to obtain.

Second, film itself is a more flexible medium than videotape. It can be edited with much greater precision so that the production personnel can exercise greater control over its final form than is usually possible with studio production.

Third, the use of film gives both producer and director greater opportunity to display their skills in producing the programmes. In this case, there was to be six weeks of research work on the series before the first programme was recorded in the studio. Until that time, filming was almost the only work which would require the special skills of a director.

Fourth, film is thought to ensure greater interest and attention from the viewer. This belief was behind the producer's idea, put forward at the first meeting, of including a short sequence of archive film at the beginning of the first programme, to 'hook' the audience. 'We know from experience that this slot on Sunday afternoon pays off best when you've got film in it. The devil of it is, of course, that archive film is very expensive per foot.'

The contact chain

The question of who should present the programmes was also raised at the first meeting. An initial choice had to be made between a subject specialist and a professional television man. Both producer and director felt a professional was necessary to handle the production smoothly on the studio floor and to carry the audience along with the subject matter. The ability of different presenters to carry the audience seemed to depend first on how well-known they were to viewers and secondly, on how much 'weight' was attached to their screen personalities. The producer wanted somebody known to be interested in political and current affairs who had opinions of his own but who was also known to be scrupulously fair in handling interviews and discussions. On the other hand, he did not want someone who would take over the editorial control of the series, directly or indirectly.

The presenter, who took the role in the series, was one of the first names mentioned. His recent work on the BBC TV series *Your Witness* had particularly impressed the producer. One of the producer's ideas for the last programme – a technique whereby the experts could call up their own evidence in the studio – had come from this series. The presenter had a reputation for maintaining balance, for being professionally competent, and also for being politically active in the past which added 'weight' to his public personality. Neither the producer, nor the director who had worked with him before, was afraid that he would interfere with the producer's work. The only doubt was whether others would have seen him in *Your Witness* and so whether he would be booked already or asking too high a fee.

Although it was based on two-decision criteria, a third factor entered crucially into the final choice of presenter. Both the producer and the presenter immediately thought of this presenter because of his recent appearance in the BBC TV series. The point is a very simple one – the production team could only make choices within the range of what was immediately known to them – but at later stages in the researching process this became a crucial factor.

It provides a third chain, the contact chain, accounting for the subject items which became available to the producer for inclusion in the programmes. One series of contacts led not just to a new subject item, but to the introduction of a new subject area to encompass it. The producer heard about Professor Henri Tajfel's research through a contact chain which started with James Halloran in Leicester, and led via Dipak Nandy to Henri Tajfel in Bristol. Because this research sounded ideal for television presentation, the producer added National Prejudice

DIAGRAM III

THE CONTACT CHAIN

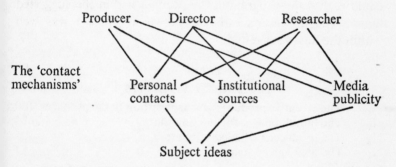

to his list of types of prejudice. A similar chain led to Dr. Pushkin who had conducted some social-psychological research on the development of prejudice among children: another suitable subject for visual presentation, as children are so photogenic.

The importance of this third chain shown in Diagram III did not fully emerge until researching on the programmes really started after these initial meetings. The role of researcher can itself be seen as an attempt to institutionalize mechanisms of contact within the production team. Researching is discussed in detail in the following chapter but first it is necessary to complete the account of agreeing the series budget.

THE BUDGET

The executive producer suggested a budget for the series based on his assessment of the amount necessary for programmes in that time-slot, balanced against the money available within the whole department. The situation within the department was not as tight as usual so the executive producer's initial suggestion was considerably higher than the normal budget figure for Sunday afternoon documentaries.

The next step was for the producer to work out the individual items in his budget with the director and to estimate whether he could realize the programmes he wanted within the suggested figure. The producer's estimate shown in Table I was well within the figure suggested.

TABLE I
THE BUDGET ESTIMATES

N_1	The executive producer's first suggestion to the producer	100
N_2	The 'usual' budget for the time-slot	75
N_3	The producer's detailed estimate	91
N_4	The final agreed figure	84

N.B. These figures are expressed as index numbers using the first budget figure as the base, 100. They are not the actual figures.

Throughout the early meetings of the production team, only the first and last programmes were differentiated from the general run of the series by specific ideas for modes of presentation. The first programme was to include a sequence of archive film demonstrating the wide variety and forms of prejudice. In the last programme, experts were to arrive at some conclusions about the phenomenon of prejudice as a whole, based on the series which had gone before. A variety of subject ideas were canvassed in discussion, but they had not yet been linked to specific programmes. Ideas about the general format appropriate dominated the way the detailed budget estimates were made. The basic strategy of the programmes was to have experts discussing previously presented evidence. This suggested a particular combination of three basic ingredients – film for the evidence, experts to discuss and a presenter to link the two together. As can be seen from the estimates shown in Table 2 these three items together accounted for just over two-thirds of the budget, with the presenter alone taking up one-third. The programme strategy was based on the expectation that the

TABLE 2

THE PRODUCER'S BUDGET ESTIMATES

	%
Presenter	33
Film unit	18
Guests and actor	17
Researcher	7
Studio equipment[1]	5
Still photographs and captions ..	4
Archive film	4
Set and scenery (total)	4
Technical costs[2]	3
Expenses (total)	3
Other	1
	99[3]

(1) Teleprompter, eidophor, etc.
(2) Cost of videotape, cameras, etc.
(3) Because of rounding the percentages do not total 100.

series would mainly be produced in the studio, because of the likely budget which went with the time-slot.

In this case production possibilities were not directly constrained by the budget so much as by beliefs about appropriate programme format based on time-slot and likely budget. Even allowing for unexpected contingencies, the detailed estimates were well within the budget figure. To the producer this meant 'either more film or more guests', but the producer and director agreed together that neither could be expanded. The budget allowed for two guests per programme and three in the last, sufficient for half-hour programmes. To do more filming would have meant finding more subjects to film; here the production process ran into another factor, *time*, which did act simply as a constraint, as shown in Table 3.

TABLE 3

PROJECTED TIMETABLE FOR PRODUCTION OF
The Nature of Prejudice

October 1967

1st two weeks	Preliminary meetings/planning
2nd two weeks	Researching for programme material

November

1st week	Filming
2nd week	Researching
3rd week	Filming
4th week	Researching
Start of 5th week	1st studio date – recording Programme I

January 1968

7th	Transmission of Programme I
18th	Studio recording of Programme VII

February

18th	Transmission of Programme VII

This was the production timetable as it appeared at the end of the second meeting, 10th October, 1967.

The importance of the time factor was illustrated by one decision made in the course of the budget discussions. In earlier planning the producer had been particularly keen to shoot some film illustrating some of the well-known centres of prejudice in Great Britain. He would have liked to have visited Northern Ireland though he felt it might be politically and economically more feasible to go to Birmingham to film what then appeared to be the worst inter-racial situation in Britain. These ideas were not mentioned at all in the first meeting and only brought up by the director in the second. The producer then ruled them out on the grounds of money and time. The subject was not reopened when they had completed the budget estimate and found that there was a surplus.

The short time in which the programmes had to be prepared

did limit what could be done. Finance is also often regarded as a limiting factor. In this case it was not so much the particular budget which limited what could be done, as past experience of handling similar programmes within the same time-slot and budget framework. Production personnel seem to work within an occupational milieu in which technical and financial constraints are already familiar and in which cultural understandings have developed on what the constraints mean for the actual handling of the processes of production. The important factor in this case was not the actual budget figure, but what budget and time-slot were thought to mean.

After the producer had prepared his estimates, the other departmental executive found out that the budget figure for the series was well above the customary budget for the time-slot. He began to question this and to take action which suggested he might move in and reduce it. This action consisted in manipulating various administrative devices under his control. One such device was the provision of an office in ATV House in which the production team could work. The possession of an office is essential for television personnel as a base from which to start collecting programme material. It is also a symbol of security. Offices change hands fairly steadily in television companies with the change in programme schedules. Stories of people turning up at their office only to find someone else occupying it, are a familiar part of media folk-lore.

Another device was thrown up by the employment of the researcher on the series. The researcher was technically on contract to ATV, not on staff. A memo was circulated to the contracts department stating that contract researchers should not be employed unless all staff researchers were fully occupied. At this time there was a staff researcher free, but both producer and director preferred their first choice. The producer felt he was particularly unfortunate in being caught between the two departmental executives, as one faction 'flexed its muscles' in the face of the other. Burns and Stalker have pointed out that the political and status systems of an organization may be independent of the working organization, even though events in one are liable to influence events in the other. In this case the budget figure was secure as the executive producer had already cleared support from higher management for his figure.

The final conference to agree the estimates between representatives of the accounts and technical services sections and the producer and director, followed a regular, apparently ritualized, pattern. The accounts representative went through the estimates item by item looking for small adjustments which could be made. One indication that no drastic reductions would be made came when the accounts representative raised the question of the filming costs. After some discussion both the producer and the director agreed that a token adjustment was possible here, in the same way as with some of the other estimates. At that point the accounts representative himself changed his position, advising them to keep the original estimate to allow for eventualities. The discussion in this conference was carried on in terms of what was 'usual', 'normal' or had been done in similar circumstances for similar productions in the past. This conference appeared to give a representative of administration and accounts the right to pronounce on programme policy. As one might expect this was resented by the 'creative' production personnel. The meeting itself, however, had little importance. The executive producer had previously contacted the executives in accounts and administration to secure their support. Moreover, the production personnel recognized that even the final agreed budget estimates were treated quite loosely by the administration. Over-spending later had to be excessive before the producer was really called to task.*

In the event the final agreed estimate (N.4 in Table 1) was 16% down on the original per-programme budget figure and 7% down on the producer's detailed estimates. The final figure,

---

* Probably more important than a reprimand was the possibility that over-spending might be taken into account when considering an individual's future employment.

however, was still some 9% higher than the 'usual' budget for a programme in this time-slot. In Table 4 the final figure has been translated back to show what it meant in terms of programme format.*

TABLE 4

TYPE OF CONTENT BUDGETED (per programme)

	Mins
Actuality film from archives and libraries ..	1
Film shot specially for the series	8–9
Presenter, studio experts, actor reading ..	20
	30

A comparison of this breakdown with the actual per-programme figures in Appendix A shows that the budget estimates were only a loose indication of final programme shape.

The Briefing Meeting

Once the detailed budget estimates had been agreed, the next meeting of the producer and director was to brief the researcher on subjects for the series. At this meeting the producer listed the substantive types of prejudice on which he wanted the others to work.

The producer recognized that the social and religious subject areas were less relevant now than they had been a few years ago. Social prejudice had been discussed at the first meeting between the producer and director. Initially, both were doubtful whether attitudes of class conflict were still current in modern Britain. The director was sceptical whether they would find people who would express hostility to the members of another class. He felt people did not think in class terms any more. The producer, however, thought they did. At the briefing meeting social prejudice was still defined in general historical terms – 'the upper class as opposed to the cloth cap working class' – but with the addition of one subject area, Nancy Mitford's famous

* This possible format was outlined by the producer. It is not simply an inference.

dissertation on 'U' and 'Non-U'. This first discussion between the producer and director was carried on in terms of personal feelings, experiences and acquaintances. The briefing meeting hardly advanced the subject beyond expression of a vague belief that this was a prejudice which had been significant in the past.

The producer was not only important in choosing the subject area but also in providing a range of knowledge and contacts to develop each area with subject ideas. The discussion within the production team was carried on in terms of personal feelings, without reference to any other evidence. Very little material on the subject of social prejudice was collected in the course of later researching and even less of this material was used in the programmes, because the production team was not clear what ideas to collect under this heading.

In contrast, when the producer put forward inter-sexual prejudice as a subject area at the briefing meeting, he touched off an immediate response from the researcher. She was interested in the subject of female emancipation anyway and had previously done some programme research on the subject. She already had a set of contacts of her own, as well as a knowledge of the topic. In later stages of the production process it became clear that some of the production team regarded prejudice against women as *passé*, in much the same way as social and religious prejudice. One of the factors which prevented it dropping out of production research, like social prejudice, was the researcher's personal interest in the subject and the contacts she could use.

Table 5 shows the origin of the six subject areas put forward at the briefing meeting. It also raises an important point about the *subject*, *presentation* and *contact* chains. Although these were conceptually and in some cases actually separate, final decisions on what subjects to research and what subjects to include in the programme depended on the composite action of all three. Material included in the programmes had to satisfy all three criteria implied in the chains. However, it was possible to assess the relative importance of each of the three chains in suggesting and reinforcing the selection of particular subject ideas, as they came up. For a subject area to be developed it had to be understood by the production team and material had to be readily available through the usual production channels to substantiate

TABLE 5

SUBJECT AREAS AT THE BRIEFING MEETING

Origin	*Area*	*Later development**
Producer – subject chain	Race and colour Inter-generational	Subject matter understood and available
Producer – subject chain	Religious	Subject matter understood and found
Producer – subject chain	Inter-sexual	Subject matter understood and available to researcher
Contact chain	National	One subject item in contact chain
Producer – subject chain	Social	Subject matter not understood and not available or found

* The distinction between 'found' and 'available' is explained in the text.

it. The distinction in Table 5 between material which was *available* and material which had to be *found*, depends on how far material was readily accessible through the *usual channels* of television researching, discussed in the following chapter.

In addition to these broad subject areas, the producer mentioned a number of different subject ideas at the briefing meeting. Some of these were examples and some items on which he hoped the researcher would actually start work. Table 6 gives examples of the way different ideas were suggested and reinforced by the three chains.

After the meeting the director commented on the fact that there were no rough programme synopses; he contrasted this

TABLE 6

SUBJECT IDEAS AT THE BRIEFING MEETING

Main origin	Reinforced by	Idea
Subject chain i.e. 1 we ought to cover 2 we could do that by	Presentation chain (such and such topic)* (such and such technique)	1 Film anthology of types of prejudice 2 Advertising boards showing discrimination 3 Multi-racial school situation
Subject chain i.e. 1 we ought to cover 2 we came across a good example of that	Contact chain (such and such topic)	1 Headteachers objecting to children's appearances 2 Pushkin's experiments on children 3 Literary examples of types of prejudice
Presentation chain i.e. 1 we ought to use 2 that would fit in with	Subject chain (such and such technique) (such and such subject)	1 'Vox Pop' (street interviews) 2 'Vox Intelligentia' (Filmed interviews with experts)
Contact chain i.e. 1 I came across 2 that would fit in with	Subject chain (such and such an item) (such and such a subject)	1 Correspondence in the *Spectator* 2 Correspondence in *The Times* 3 Woman engineer's inability to obtain employment
Contact chain i.e. 1 I came across 2 we could do that by	Presentation chain (such and such an item) (such and such technique)	1 Tajfel's experiments with children

* The forms of argument quoted in each section are only *illustrative*. As mentioned above, items actually included in the programmes had to satisfy all three conditions. The important point is the different orders of priority shown in the origins.

with his own previous production experience. In the past he had always thought rough programme synopses a pre-requisite to the allocation of a budget. Both he and the researcher felt overwhelmed by the mass of material available. They both assumed that the producer had thought the subject through and would provide the necessary structuring within which they could set about collecting material.

The subject chain played an important role in guiding the researcher in her task of collecting material. After the briefing meeting she expected to base her investigations on the six subject areas put forward by the producer.

Researcher: . . . coming in at this stage I feel completely lost. There is so much material around, I don't know where to begin. My feeling is to jump in and start ringing everyone up, but I think it will come out a lot better if I just sit and think about it and try to sort it out myself for a while.

Observer: How will you set about sorting it out?

Researcher: Well, there are these six categories I was given in the material already. I think they will obviously form the basis. Then I will try and get material under each heading. I mean, the material we will need will come in pretty well-defined types – interviews, experts, studio work – that sort of thing . . .

This conversation shows the way in which the presentation chain and the contact chain also set the framework within which the researcher operated. The researcher was already thinking in terms of material suitable for presentation in ways which would fit the programme format. Her reference to telephoning is an important indication of the type and range of available contacts. Television researchers gradually build up a telephone and address book full of potentially useful contacts. These books are the capital with which they work.

This discussion of the briefing meeting is a first example of the way in which the selection and gathering of programme items depended heavily on the ideas and contacts built up by the production team through their past experience, and on the contacts which they could activate immediately in the period of researching for the programmes. Neither of these sets of contacts could be expected to provide an exhaustive or even a comprehensive survey of possible material. They depended heavily on largely fortuitous processes such as personal acquaintance. The importance of personal relationships and contacts in the whole production process is a recurrent theme of this case study which is taken up again in the following chapter.

3

Collecting programme material

As soon as work on the programmes started, the contact chain acquired much greater importance as a source of subject ideas. Within the contact chain three particular mechanisms may be distinguished as the 'usual channels' through which suitable material became visible to the production team. These mechanisms were the press, organizations and associations representing particular interest groups, and personal acquaintances. Table 1 shows the primary source of the subject ideas, discussed within the production team during the first week's researching. More than half of these were generated through the three contact mechanisms.

Table 1 also reflects the pattern of interaction within the production team at this time. The director was acting, as he put it, as supernumerary researcher, but he was anxious not to poach on the researcher's territory. He confined his interests largely to the selection of film material. The producer had already laid down general guidelines. It was the researcher's job to come up with both material and ideas during this researching period. There was considerable scope at this stage for the researcher to bring new ideas and material to the producer's attention in the office. But many of these ideas had no more than a single airing.

The list of subject areas shown in Table 2 increased to eight during the first week. Stereotypes were introduced by the producer as a separate area with the idea that they might be

TABLE 1

THE SOURCES OF SUBJECT IDEAS IN THE FIRST WEEK

Primary source*	No of ideas
Press	7
Organization	7
Researcher contact	5
Researcher idea	9
Producer idea	1
	29

*In discussion within the production team, one idea inevitably led to another. For this table only the first idea in such chains has been counted.

illustrated by feature film clips and cartoons from comics. At this time the producer was reading Allport's general survey of *The Nature of Prejudice* and the last set of programme outlines,

TABLE 2

SUBJECT AREAS AND SUBJECT IDEAS IN THE FIRST WEEK

Area	No of ideas
Race and colour	11
Religious	6
Inter-sexual	4
Inter-generational	2
Social	4
National	1
Minorities	6
Stereotypes	5
	39*

*For this table, all discrete ideas have been counted, not simply the primary ideas as in Table 1.

prepared in the adult education phase, both of which emphasized stereotyping among other features of prejudice. The second additional subject area was minority groups. This was never explicitly defined or added to the list by the production team but it emerged as a separate area through the process of finding interview subjects, discussed below. Table 2 shows that although race and colour was the largest area, it did not at this stage overwhelmingly dominate the other areas. This was because the researcher made a determined effort to seek out material under the other headings, especially religious and social. Much of this material was not used at later stages because the producer thought it did not really come within the topic of prejudice.

RESEARCHING FILM SUBJECTS

The production team were working to a tight timetable. Their first aim was to line up enough subjects to keep a camera crew occupied in the third production week.* Considerations of cost as well as crew morale required that something should be ready for filming on the days for which the crew were hired. For this reason the 'Vox Pop' sequences were placed at the start of the filming programme. Nothing had to be done to arrange these sequences beyond picking locations and clearing permission with the local police. The choice of locations involved such practical questions as the width of the pavement, the general level of traffic noise and the proximity of cover in case of rain and also some consideration of the type of people likely to pass the spot, in particular the proportion of coloured immigrants to be expected.

The producer gave a new slant to his directives when he asked the researcher to look for people who could be interviewed on film. These were to be either victims of prejudice who could tell their own story, or people with strongly prejudiced views who would be prepared to state them on the record. The process of contacting people produced a number of interviewees who did not come within any of six subject areas already outlined. An ex-prisoner, a homosexual and a lesbian were all contacted by the researcher through organizations representing these minorities; a gipsy and a spokesman for

* See production calendar p. 36

gipsies were reached after a story about gipsies had appeared in the national press. From previous work on another programme the researcher had a personal contact with a lady running a Social Welfare Agency in Notting Hill. The researcher approached her in the hope of finding interviewees who would be able to recount their own experience as victims of prejudice. These examples show the use of all three contact mechanisms. Representative organizations were particularly important in developing the separate subject area of minority groups. In general terms the reasons for contacting particular organizations ranged from the feeling that a 'courtesy call' was necessary (Institute of Race Relations), through a wish to investigate a specific case (Institute of Women Engineers) to a hope that they would be a fruitful source of material (Campaign against Racial Discrimination, Woman's Society for the Anglican Ministry). On the first morning the producer picked up no less than three items through the second contact mechanism, the morning papers. These were the repercussions of a recent survey of gipsies by the Ministry of Housing and Local Government, a case of discrimination against a woman engineer and a report of a Parish magazine article in which the vicar expressed strong anti-semitic sentiments. All three contact mechanisms frequently involved a long chain of sources before a possible interviewee was reached. The distinction between the three mechanisms is clearer analytically than it was in practice.

Table 3 shows that while interviewees were fairly evenly distributed by source, the distribution by subject area was heavily weighted to race and colour. The table is slightly misleading in the presentation of sources. All the seven 'personal source' interviewees were contacted through the same source – the social worker in Notting Hill. Moreover, even primary sources overlap. The two interviewees on inter-generational prejudice, added in the later filming session, were both contacted through the same organization, the Arts Laboratory. But this organizational contact was only fruitful because of the personal contacts of one member of the production team.

TABLE 3

INTERVIEWEES BY PRIMARY SOURCE AND SUBJECT*

Subject	*Source*			
	Press	*Organization*	*Personal*	*Total*
Race/colour	4	1 (2)	7	12 (2)
Religious (inc. anti-semitism)	1	1	—	2
Inter-sexual	1	—	—	1
Inter-generational	—	— (2)	—	0 (2)
Social	—	—	—	0
National	—	—	—	0
Minority groups	2	3	—	5
	8	5 (4)	7	20 (4)
Unclassifiable† or filmed separately				3
Interviews filmed Total				27

* All figures refer to the first week's filming except those in brackets which were interviews added a fortnight later. Primary source of contact means the source for the first mention of the subject idea. Thus for example the gipsies (referred to in the text) are attributed to the press and not to organizations.

† The primary source for one case was unclear.

The preponderance of interviewees concerned with race and colour was a simple consequence of the fact that the word 'prejudice' naturally suggested this to the production team and to those with whom they came in contact. All the Notting Hill Social Worker's contacts came within this subject area. Further examples appear below of the way in which outside contacts, upon whom the production team depended for material, tended to equate 'prejudice' and 'colour'. The four additional interviewees, filmed during an extra day's filming, were picked specifically to fill gaps in the material which was already available from the first week. As can be seen in Table 3, two of the additional interviewees illustrated inter-generational prejudice. This had not previously been covered. The other two were representatives of the Black Power Movement, a movement which the producer thought showed that prejudice is 'two sides of the same penny.'* Among the interviews already filmed a Jamaican landlord told of prejudice and hostility between West Indians from different islands, and an Irishman told of discrimination against the Irish which sounded word for word like the account of a coloured person's troubles. The producer was particularly pleased to have these on film because they were unusual variations on the common theme. He hoped they might surprise the audience by showing them that the phenomenon was more widespread than they had thought – that prejudice was even present among those who were conventionally thought of as its victims.

The bulk of the non-race and colour interviewees came within the minority group area. One reason for this concentration was that minority groups were readily available through the contact mechanisms, a second that the producer particularly wanted to get examples of the victims of prejudice; and a third that the researcher and director were collecting material with only a vague idea of the definition of prejudice. In the first weeks there was considerable, often humorous, debate between the two of them on what was and what was not prejudice.

At the end of the first week the researcher reported back to the producer. He made a number of *ad hoc* decisions as to what were examples of prejudice. The researcher hoped to get some idea of whether she was working along the right lines. Their conversation moved from a discussion of relevant authors and books to specific examples of prejudice which the researcher wanted to check. These included religious instruction in schools, the Lord's Day Observance Society and the deference to be found among some members of the working class. These were all rejected by the producer as not really prejudice. Finally he was drawn to attempt a partial definition – that a readily recognizable group of people must be involved as victims, and

---

* For reasons which will become apparent later the actual film of this interview was not used to fulfil the original intention of showing that white prejudice was mirrored by black prejudice.

that the attitude must be irrational. The researcher took up this point of irrationality by quoting a letter written by Sir Cyril Osborne to a newspaper, which appeared to be both rational and prejudiced.* The producer's answer was that a prejudiced person would continue to hold the same opinion, even if his argument was shown to be false. It was easiest for the production team to resolve the ambiguity surrounding the concept of 'prejudice' by thinking in terms of people exposed to it and the hostile relationship between the members of different groups: 'in-groups' and 'out-groups'. They were guided in that direction by the producer. Only two interviewees were found in the three general areas which did not themselves entail an obvious group of victims—religious, social and national. The only subject area gap actually filled in the second film session was the inter-generational area, where prejudice had an obvious referent – long-haired youths.

Many more of the interviews conducted on film were with victims of prejudice than with actual prejudiced people. Table 4 shows that only three interviewees actually expressed prejudiced opinions and all of these were contacted through press reports. The victims of prejudice were more visible to the television production team, for example through the protective associations, than prejudiced people themselves. There are a limited number of public platforms through which individuals can make their own prejudices known. Two of the three who were interviewed were vicars whose job gave them privileged access to a public forum. On the other hand, no attempt was made to contact extremists from any of the British neo-fascist parties or from extreme racialist groups; apparently because of a taboo on allowing people with that sort of view any chance at all of putting it over on the medium. This is in spite of the fact that these interviews were recorded on film and only used afterwards in small snippets, giving the producer complete control over the output.

* Sir Cyril Osborne was later invited to appear in the first version of Programme VI as an example of a prejudiced individual. See Chapter 5.

TABLE 4

INTERVIEWEES BY SUBJECT AND TYPE

Subject	Type*			
	Prejudiced persons	*Victims representatives*	*Research workers experienced*	*Total*
Race/Colour	2–(2)†–	7	3	12 (2)
Religious (inc. anti-semitism)	1	2	—	3
Inter-sexual	—	1	—	1
Inter-generational	—	— (2)	—	0 (2)
Social	—	—	—	0
National	—	—	—	0
Minority	—	5	—	5
	3–(2)–	15 (2)	3	21 (4)

Two Race/Colour 'experienced' filmed separately   2

Interviewees filmed total 27

* These categories are explained in the text below.
† These two interviewees, as explained in the text, were both Black Power representatives. They were originally included with the idea they would themselves be examples of prejudice, but they were in fact interviewed mainly as victims and representatives.

TABLE 5

INTERVIEWEES BY TYPE AND PRIMARY SOURCE

Source	Type			
	Prejudiced person	*Victim representative*	*Research worker experienced*	*Total*
Press	3	3	2	8
Organization	—–(2)*–	5 (2)	—	5 (4)
Personal	—	6	2	8
	3	14 (2)	4	21 (4)
			Unclassifiable	2
			Interviewees filmed total	27

* See note † to Table 4.

A third group of people interviewed on film were the *research workers* and *experienced* who were able to report more generally on the racial situation from either their research work or their professional experiences.* Both the two research workers were contacted through press stories on the publication of their research. One study was of an industrial dispute in Southall, which had involved a large number of Indian workers; the other a survey of the British housing market. The authors of both these studies were recruited because their studies were in the right field and happened to come out at the right moment, i.e. during the two week researching period.

The two *experienced* interviewees† were the headmistresses of the two schools, used as locations in which to film the two social-psychological experiments and to record the activities of children in a multi-racial school environment. The first school, Yerbury Road Primary School in North London, was picked as a result of a contact chain which led the producer to Miss Arthur, the headmistress of the school. He then went on to make contact with the staff of the school to gain their cooperation. He was particularly pleased to find that one member of the staff remembered meeting him at a party given by a mutual acquaintance.

Once the producer had prepared the way through these personal visits, he had to go through the machinery of the Inner London Education Authority to get formal permission to film in the school. As there are a large number of broadcasting and film teams working in London, the Education Authority has come to exercise close control over the use of the children in its schools. The initial response to the producer's letter was a straight 'no'. This refusal simply reflected the generally restrictive policy of the Authority. The producer's reaction was to try to circumvent the formal channels by a

* These are terms used only in this study and not by the production team. They are used to avoid describing these five as 'experts' because that term is better reserved for guests invited into the studio to appear 'live'.
† These two interviewees are the ones recorded as being 'filmed separately' in Tables 3 and 4.

direct approach to a member of the authority who had himself worked in television. Permission to film at Yerbury Road was eventually given, but only on certain conditions. No experiments were to be filmed which might suggest that a child had a preference for one colour or another. Because racial tension was a particularly sensitive political point, the Education Authority did not want any suggestion made that there was less than complete harmony in their schools.*

The conditions set by the Authority meant that although it was possible to film scenes of children at play at Yerbury Road, there was still no school in which to film Dr. Pushkin's and Professor Tajfel's experiments. Another way round the Education Authority's ruling was to approach schools outside their jurisdiction – private schools. The headmistress of the first private school picked from the telephone directory agreed to cooperate immediately. She was only too pleased for the filming to be carried out on the following Tuesday afternoon, the time at which it had been planned to film Dr. Pushkin's experiments at the Yerbury Road School.

The contrast between the reactions of the two schools was thus very marked. On the one hand television presentation was seen as a possible threat, on the other as a means to publicity and prestige with pupils and parents.

RESEARCHING ARCHIVE FILM

A number of film libraries in London keep historical collections of newsreel film. The producer intended to build a series of newsreel items into a film sequence for the first programme demonstrating the wide variety of prejudice current in different societies. To collect this material the producer could either go direct to the film libraries or contact them through ATV's own Film Department, a less productive method, because it involved

* Dr. Pushkin confirmed that the same considerations made access to London schools well-nigh impossible for social scientists wishing to conduct research on problems of race and prejudice.

a number of extra stages between the producer and the actual library. Looked at as systems of information recall, the film libraries depend very heavily on the librarians. Production personnel believe the library cataloguing systems to be out of date and unreliable. Catalogue classifications do not fit the particular interests of any particular production team. Moreover, thumbing through catalogues can take up a good deal of time. The librarian can short cut all these problems for a producer, but because of this librarians tend to find themselves at the beck and call of production personnel, anxious about film for their particular programme. This can lead to tension, especially as the librarians are relatively poorly paid and have low status within the occupational milieu of television.

In his initial requests to the libraries for film for *The Nature of Prejudice*, the producer stressed the need to cover other types of prejudice, as well as race and colour. He also mentioned a number of specific instances of prejudice from the past outside the race and colour field which might have been recorded on film. But the actual selection of film material from the library archives depended to a great extent on chance factors. The initial reaction of the film librarians was that 'prejudice' meant colour now, and fascism before the war. The material available to the producer depended on the librarian's understanding of what was required from him, as well as on his knowledge of the material actually available in his library. To supplement this the producer had to rely on his own memory of past incidents or film clips he had seen in the past. The time factor prevents the film librarians becoming too closely involved with any particular programme, but in this case the producer was suspicious that they might exercise a quasi-editorial function. He suspected a reluctance to admit that there might be examples of prejudice occurring now within the United Kingdom. A producer's desire to use the librarians to get as close to the available film material as possible tends to put the librarian into the position of having to make quasi-

C

editorial judgements. This is another source of tension in the relationship.*

The producer had adopted stereotypes as a new subject area partly because it lent itself to visual illustration, in particular through feature film clips. One source for these was the library of the British Film Institute. The director had once worked with John Huntley, the Director of the BFI. A personal approach to the BFI was believed to be specially valuable because the formal channels through which film might be obtained from the Institute's library were renowned as being unworkable. Instead of simply supplying film clips, John Huntley became a collaborator in the production of a part of a programme given over to stereotyping in films. The producer described in general terms the idea he had in mind and then left John Huntley to fill in the ideas and to suggest illustrations. John Huntley was thus not simply a *source*, as were the newsreel librarians, but rather an *expert*. The difference was that while an *expert* was allowed, indeed expected, to exercise editorial judgement over his own contribution, a *source* was not expected to play any editorial part.

CONCLUSION

This chapter has dealt mainly with the intensive researching carried out in the first two production weeks. Researching continued throughout the production period and the researcher continued to work with the team until January, when the first programme was broadcast. But as the programmes developed outline structures, research became a less sweeping operation, more a process of finding particular items to fit specific holes.†

In Chapter 1 the point was made that production for tele-

* Apart from two newsreel libraries, some other sources of education film were also investigated, in the end to no purpose.

† Photograph libraries and similar sources of printed material were used later in much the same way as the film libraries described above. Apart from these, the only type of researching which has not already been mentioned, was the recruitment of guest experts for studio appearances, discussed below in Chapter 5.

vision not only takes place within the framework of large organizations, but also involves the cooperation and collaboration of a variety of production personnel to make any individual programme. When the production team met to start work on *The Nature of Prejudice* none of them had worked together before. They shared a common background from past work in television and all had worked previously within the same programme company. Understandings of usual methods of production and appropriate role behaviour were shared among the production team based on their common experience. Nevertheless, there were also elements of conflict and tension. Different role expectations, different ideas about appropriate methods of work were available within the occupational milieu.

The producer played a creative role in the production of this series in the sense that he expected to arrive at his own formulation of the problem of prejudice. To achieve this he was dependent not only on himself, his own knowledge and experience, but also on others in the production team and others at even further remove from the production of the actual programmes, from whom the necessary material had to be collected.

Analytically four relationships seem possible between a producer and those he uses to provide material. There may be complete congruence between producer and source. This is most likely to occur when the material required is highly specific. An example of such congruence was when the producer of *The Nature of Prejudice* used the ATV Film Department to obtain known film clips from known sources.

The three other relationships between a producer and his sources are all cases where a producer may not be able to realize his ideas exactly, because of the need to use intermediaries. Some sources may simply be unable or unwilling to provide the required material. For example, the Inner London Education Authority was unwilling to allow the use of its schools for *The Nature of Prejudice*. Theoretically more interesting, however, are the two remaining cases where the intermediaries or the source fail to understand the exact nature of the producer's demands or where they intentionally or unintentionally provide some other material. The film librarians had their own ideas on what constituted examples of prejudice. They provide an example of incomplete understanding between producer and source which effectively structured what was available for use in the programmes. Even within the core production team, ambiguities surrounding the definition of prejudice were a continual source of difficulty in making selection decisions.

The fourth type of relationship between producer and source is illustrated by spokesmen for the Black Power movement. In these cases the material found was different from the material sought. The producer hoped to make the point that white prejudice and black prejudice were 'two sides of the same penny'. He also viewed a newsreel clip of an interview with Malcolm X, the American Black Power leader, looking for militant statements to illustrate the same point. Neither the two representatives filmed, nor Malcolm X in the newsreel interview made the expected emotional, militant or prejudiced statements. None of the film of Malcolm X was used and the material from the specially filmed interviews was used for a different purpose, to provide another view on various aspects of the racial situation in Britain. The producer asked one of these interviewees directly whether he thought coloured people were now prejudiced against whites. The reply, which was phrased in moderate terms, justified coloured people's attitudes by reference to the experience of the Jews and the need to combat white racialism. This section of the interview was not used in the programme.

To be selected, material must usually meet the producer's expectations. The Black Power material did not meet the producer's expectations but these had been at least partly formed by the previous accounts of the Black Power movement given in the media. It could have been edited to provide a different account, but the producer did not use the material for that purpose. These examples raise again a problem discussed in another case study of the way in which events are selected and reported through the media to fit a limited number of self-supporting themes and images.* The result is to limit the number of 'views of the world' available in society. But these examples also show that this phenomenon is embedded in the relationship between production and source. One reason for following accepted interpretations of events is that the alternative account may have been put forward as a deliberate attempt to mislead. But in this time there was no evidence in these cases that the Black Power representatives had set out to do so and the interview with Malcolm X had been previously recorded for another purpose.

But as well as limiting what the producers could achieve, the mechanisms used to contact sources themselves played a part in structuring the content of the production. The three general contact mechanisms identified in the course of this chapter were the press, associations representing people or causes related to the subject matter and the personal contacts of the production team. An example of the way in which these structured available content occurred in the selection of the two 'research workers' for interview through the press. These studies and not others appeared in the programmes, because they had been completed at the right time to be reported. The other research studies actually re-created on film for use in the programmes were thrown up through the different mechanism of personal contact. In both cases the use of contact mechanisms generated a limited sample of content. Other studies, perhaps as relevant, or even more relevant, were not considered because they were not visible.

There is a general tendency within television production to use and value personal, particularistic relationships. Various examples of the use of personal approaches in researching for *The Nature of Prejudice* suggest that such approaches are not only more productive, or believed to be more so by television personnel, but also that they play a part in reflecting status

* See note 3 to Chapter 8, p. 166.

within the social system of television production. Personal contacts are thought to be more productive because:

1   The producer* can interest and personally involve the contact in meeting his requirements, which can be explained in detail if necessary.

2   The producer can judge whether the contact will produce material suitable for presentation on television.

3   The producer is in closer touch with the material and thus can prevent the contact usurping his own functions by making editorial judgements or by giving only brief details.

4   The producer can hope to get more cooperation from the contact than would be likely using a purely contractual relationship. This cooperation may be practical – for example, a location in which to film – or may involve the contact in giving his own ideas on possible material.

5   The producer does not have expert knowledge of the subject but must rely on obtaining such knowledge quickly in a condensed and usable form.

6   Personal contacts can be used to allay suspicions about the motives behind the television presentation and the possible uses to which it may be put.

7   These suspicions are generally strongest in approaches to public bodies or formally organized bodies with developed status hierarchies. These same bodies also tend to work through formal processes of contact which they can easily block.

8   Formal processes of contact generally take time and the producer may be unfamiliar with the exact way they should be handled to produce the best results.

9   Access through formal channels is potentially open to anyone. The producer is aiming to create an individual

* 'The producer' in this list means any or all members of the production team.

set of programmes, differentiated by the material which he puts into them. One way of obtaining differentiated material is to use personal contacts which are not potentially open to everyone.

10 The stress on personal contacts with sources parallels the predominance of personalized relationships within the production organizations.*

11 Especially for the researcher, the ability to make and use contacts is an important part of the production role. Knowing who to go to shows competence in the work.

12 Some contacts value an approach from television. In those cases the producer is doing them a favour and he may be able to build up and use a stock of informal goodwill which will be both useful and flattering. Working for television is publicly visible and 'glamorous'. Making personal contacts to get cooperation has the latent consequence of making the producer aware of this.†

The first five reasons show why personal contacts are believed to be productive *per se*. Of these, the first four apply generally to all types of contacts and the fifth reason applies especially to those contacts with expert knowledge. Points 6–9 stress their value over more formal types of contact. From a different angle, points 10–12 show that personal contacts can be seen as part of a more general system of status and exchange within television production.

In later chapters it will be argued that there is an important tendency for television to be a reflective medium, sampling the range of conventional wisdom available in society on any topic and then relaying it back to society in programme form. Elaboration of this argument must await further evidence from later stages of the production process. Nevertheless, it is im-

* This point is taken up in Chapter 7 below, especially in relation to career prospects and employment opportunities.
† As should be clear from the above discussion not all contacts have this consequence. Suspicious contacts are better approached personally for the different reason (no. 6) mentioned above.

portant to emphasize that the purpose of introducing it is not so much critical as analytical. Reflection of the conventional wisdom could be made into a justification of communication media in functionalist terms.* For the moment it is only necessary to show how all three of the generalizations about television production elaborated in this concluding section support the argument that television is liable to be reflective. The co-operative and collaborative enterprise of production and the need to use outside sources and intermediaries make it difficult to adopt a definition of a problem varying widely from the common beliefs in society shared by all those involved in the process. Rather it seems likely that there will be an unavoidable tendency to follow such beliefs. Similarly, the way in which the three contact mechanisms generate particular types of programme content and the general stress placed on personal relationships seems to have the latent consequence that programme content will develop within frameworks of meaning widely shared and available, which form the most important part of a distinctively media culture.

In this chapter our attention has been focused on researching, the stage in the production process in which the contact chain and its subsidiary mechanisms were of particular importance. We must now examine further the workings of the subject and presentation chains in the preparation of programme outlines and scripts.

---

* Indeed, the current chairman of the Independent Television Authority, Lord Aylestone, has argued that television should reflect and follow but not lead. The application of functionalist theory to the media in society was discussed in Chapter 1.

4

Preparing programme outlines and scripts

The producer himself wrote the scripts for *The Nature of Prejudice*. The scripts themselves were preceded by a number of oral and written, outlines and ideas which helped to guide the collection of programme material, and so to structure what was available. Then the producer wrote the scripts from the collected material.

The consecutive stages of the production process are summarized in Table 1. The stages overlapped in time and each developed on what had gone before, but they can be separated for analysis. This chapter is mainly concerned with the three central stages, leading up to the preparation of detailed outlines and scripts. The outlines and scripts in particular can be seen as an important watershed; in the course of production the programmes developed various forms of objective existence which tended to commit the production team to later developments.* Up to the time they appeared, programme material had been collected within loose instructions, using the three mechanisms of the contact chain. Later, however, the scripts and outlines provided an explicit structure which set the seal on what each programme would be like.

Written and Oral Input

The producer played the central part in selecting and ordering the various programme inputs summarized in Table 2. Aca-

* See note 35 to Chapter I, p. 21.

demic knowledge, using the term broadly to cover all written material, was a much less important component in documentary than in educational production. Much of the academic knowledge which was taken into account for the programmes, for example, the producer's background reading, was not used directly, but exercised a more general influence.*

The use made of the two social-psychological experiments recorded on film illustrates the problems of incorporating

TABLE I

THE STAGES OF THE PROGRAMME PRODUCTION PROCESS

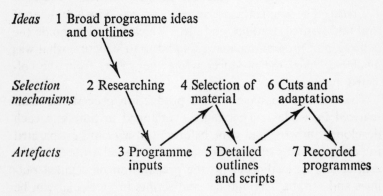

academic knowledge into the programmes. Within the production team, the justifications given for including these experiments ranged from the value of the substantive findings of the research to the photogenic qualities of the particular experiments and their usefulness in illustrating research and methods. In the briefing meeting, for example, the main reason given for including the research was that it was very suitable for filming, but the production team showed some interest in what had been discovered through the experiments. During the filming of the actual experiments, the director in particular

* The main items of background reading were Allport's *The Nature of Prejudice*, Adorno *et al's The Authoritarian Personality*, *The Street Report* on Legislation against Racial Discrimination and the PEP Survey of *Racial Discrimination in Britain*.

became very sceptical about the methods used and the value of any findings. The producer agreed that they were only using this research as an illustration. However, once both experiments were recorded on film they acquired something of the status of established fact. Moreover, they were established facts without any research or academic context. In later discussions reference

TABLE 2

MAIN INPUTS TO *The Nature of Prejudice*
PROGRAMME OUTLINES

		Type of input	Main type of use*
1	*Written and oral*	Background reading	Diffuse
		Conversation with academic contacts	Diffuse
		Programme adviser's outlines from adult education phase	Diffuse and specific
		Dr. Pushkin's and Professor Tajfel's Research	Specific
2	*Visual*	Vox Pop Interviews	Specific
		Individual Interviews	Specific
		School Location Film	Specific
		Experiments Film	Specific
		Newsreel Film	Specific

* Diffuse means they influenced the producer in a general way. Specific means actual pieces were abstracted for use in programmes.

was made to Dr. Pushkin's findings, as if these were the final statements on children and racial attitudes. For example, in the first summary outlines for Programmes I and II Dr. Pushkin's research was billed as follows:

Programme II

'Recapitulation of question on the age at which prejudice manifests itself. What research in this country has shown: film: (the Pushkin experiment).'

The production team's ambivalent attitude to academic work led eventually to some confusion in the way the actual results were given to the viewer.* In summary, three factors lay behind the selection of academic research for the programmes: the producer's prior knowledge and the contacts he made, the photogenic qualities of the material itself, and its visibility during the researching period.

THE FILMED INPUT—INTERVIEWS

Unlike much of the academic input, the filmed input could be traced through the successive stages of production as a distinct body of material which was gradually selected and ordered for programme presentation. Initially, as described in the previous chapter, contact was made with possible film subjects; then the producer selected which subjects were actually to be filmed and this was carried out; finally, selections were made from the filmed material and these were incorporated into the programme scripts.

The producer carried out the interviews himself using a different approach with each of the three different types of interviewee. From the 'victims' of prejudice he wanted personal accounts of their experiences of prejudice. From the 'prejudiced' people, he wanted clear statements of the prejudices they held. From the 'experienced' he wanted their views and accounts of their experiences. A fourth line of approach was added when the director suggested that they should use the time between interviews to encourage interviewees to enlarge generally on their views about prejudice. The producer prepared the ground beforehand with each interviewee, but in some cases prompting was necessary. For example, if an interviewee simply answered 'Yes' to a complex question, the 'Yes' could not stand alone in later edited sequences. The interviews were all filmed with the interviewer completely out of shot. The intention was not to

* See Chapter 6 for some research evidence on this point.

show him on the screen or to use his questions, but to build up the programme outlines simply by using interviewee statements.

In one case, that of an ex-prisoner, prompting took a different form: the interviewee was too over-awed by the camera and lights to be able to answer coherently for himself. The producer and the director tried to school him in phrases which would express the ideas he had discussed with them earlier. This was largely unsuccessful and the film of that particular interview was virtually useless. The production team recognized that the border line between 'putting words into someone's mouth' and 'obtaining a more coherent statement' was a narrow one.

The first film session coincided with one of a series of comedy programmes, starring John Bird, which showed the making of an imaginary television series about an unemployed man. The programme showed how the 'reality' presented on the screen was fabricated to fit the visual demands of the cameraman and the director. The camera crew appreciated this comment on their work and some felt it applied to some of the interviews already shot for *The Nature of Prejudice*. The producer, however, thought it was quite legitimate to arrange for interviewees to give answers which both expressed their meaning and were readily usable.

Throughout the filming sessions the director's main concern was to ensure that there would be pictorial variety in the eventual programmes by varying the background to each interview or the camera angle. Most interviews were shot from a horizontal or slightly raised camera position. The three 'prejudiced' people, however, were all shot from a low camera angle. The director was here following the technique which had been used with such effect by German cameramen filming Hitler. The director assumed that the audience would recognize the symbolism. This incident shows the production team using a particular technique with a particular effect in mind. But the justification for the effect was linked to symbols and techniques current within filming itself. The central reason for adopting the technique was not that the technique would have the desired effect on the audience, but that the audience would recognize the comparison with earlier techniques.

School locations

Opportunities for pictorial variety greatly increased when the filming moved to the multi-racial school at Yerbury Road. Most of the pictures to be taken there were simply *cinema verité* shots of children at work and play. The director inspected the set up but on this occasion it was the cameraman who chose which incidents to film. On his earlier visit to the school the producer had noticed that there was a good aerial view of the children in the playground from the windows of the staff room. By placing a camera there, it was possible to 'zoom in' on the children at play to introduce the film sequence and to 'zoom out' for a closing sequence.

At the other school, arrangements had to be made to film reconstructions of the two experiments. In Dr. Pushkin's study, the child was asked to choose, from a row of black and white dolls representing his or her friends, those whom he would most like to invite to a tea party. The chosen dolls were then sat at a table in an open dolls' house. Beside the table was an adult doll to represent the child's mother. The producer wanted an illustrative film sequence concentrating on pictures of the acts of choice themselves. The cameraman set up the camera in a position from which he could only film the dolls, not the child's face. When the first child began to ask 'Where is my daddy?', the cameraman protested to the director and the producer that he must film the child's face. The cameraman was thinking in terms of the human interest of the visual images. In contrast, the producer was more concerned about the information content of the sequence. On this occasion the difference of opinion was not acrimonious and a compromise was easily arranged. This was one of the clearest instances of the cameraman playing a part in deciding the shape of the film.

There was also a difference of opinion over the filming of

Professor Tajfel's research, which involved Professor Tajfel himself. Again the producer simply wanted illustrative film of children using the experimental equipment; he did not feel that the children should follow the experiment through according to the rigorous psychological methodology used in the original research. Professor Tajfel, however, was worried that the film might suggest that there were elementary flaws in the methodology. The research involved children sorting photographs of young white males into five categories ranging from 'I like him very much' to 'I dislike him very much'. In a second stage, they sorted the same photographs into two boxes labelled 'English' and 'Not English'. The child needed an interviewer to guide him through these tasks, but whereas in the actual research the instructions used by the interviewers had been carefully randomized, this could not be done on the afternoon of the filming.

Professor Tajfel was still concerned about this when he saw the edited film sequence. In the programme (No. IV of the series) the sequence was followed by a studio conversation between the presenter, and Professor Tajfel. This began as follows:

Presenter: Dr. Tajfel, that was a fascinating experiment. Now what was the point of it?

Professor Tajfel: Well, that experiment was really a bit of a gimmick. We know, of course, a great deal about the history of nationalist ideas in Europe . . . (goes on to explain the ideas behind the experiment).

Professor Tajfel's first sentence was intended to disassociate the filmed experiment from those which he had actually conducted. The remark was later edited out of the final version of the programme because the producer thought that, as it stood, it appeared to deprecate the whole idea of the experiment – not just the experiment as it had been recorded on film.

Cutting and editing

Cutting and editing were carried out in the ATV film department. The film editor and his assistant assigned to the series, worked to instructions from the producer and director.

These varied in precision according to the subject of the film. Once the producer had described where he would be using each piece, what it was intended to illustrate, and at what length, these pieces were handed over to the film editor to edit into visually attractive sequences. The film editor was left a fairly free hand to edit the sequences of children playing at the Yerbury Road School, and the two illustrative pieces on the experiments. The film editor seemed to pick out and emphasize in editing, the same type of shots that the cameraman had specially tried for in shooting the film. For example, in the playground the cameraman had followed several particular groups of children, including one solitary child who appeared to be a 'loner'. The film editor picked this child out as well for the final sequence. Similarly, in making up the sequence on Dr. Pushkin's research, the film editor used many of the shots showing the children's faces, which the cameraman had made a special effort to film. These examples suggest that given a constant stream of similar activity, selection will concentrate on elements of variety. Instances where a person's motives or feelings can be recognized provide one such element of variety. Most of the children in the playground were simply children at play, but seeing the 'loner' allowed one to recognize his emotions as well as his actions.

The film editor worked to much more precise instructions when editing the 'Vox Pop' and individual interview pieces. The interview sound tracks were all transcribed and marked up by the producer during the viewing session. The producer intended to blend particular points and statements made by the interviewees into the general argument of each programme, so that selection from the filmed interviews and making up the programme outlines and scripts were mutually interdependent processes. The outlines had to be written round the available interview material, while the interviews had been carried out with reference to what the programmes might eventually contain.

At the first viewing session, the producer outlined his plans for the series to the film editor. The first two programmes had been sketched on paper on production day 7 and the two other programmes existed as ideas upon which the production team was currently working. Programme I was to include two 'Vox Pop' compilations – one showing people recounting the prejudices which they themselves held; the other giving the public's own definitions of prejudice. Several of the individual interviewees had also been asked to give their definitions of prejudice. The newsreel film designed to show the different forms prejudice had taken in different societies was also to be included in Programme I. The programme was to end by raising the question of the relationship between children's attitudes and those held by their parents. This topic was to lead into the subject of the second programme, 'where does prejudice come from in children?' which was to include the film from the Yerbury Road School and Dr. Pushkin's experiment. One of the last two programmes in the series was to discuss the relative merits of education and legislation in combating prejudice. Another programme, probably the fourth, was to cover the question of 'in-groups' and 'out-groups'.

The producer only outlined these four programmes to the film editor, but two other programme ideas had been discussed within the production team by this stage. These were a programme on stereotypes, to include the sequence by John Huntley, and the film of Professor Tajfel's experiment, and the final programme was planned as a general discussion between experts.

The newsreel film was to be used in very short pieces, edited together to form a longer sequence to illustrate the variety of current prejudices. The producer wanted pieces which would make a good visual point briefly without the need for lengthy explanation in the commentary. He also wanted to ensure enough variety in the subject matter. The film sequence was intended to attract the viewer's attention, so he instructed the film editor to pick out scenes of action and violence that would make an arresting sequence.

TABLE 3

THE DRAMATIC STRUCTURE OF THE NEWSREEL
FILM SEQUENCE, PROGRAMME I

Order of items	Scenes of interpersonal violence *	Abuse of property	Non-violent
1	Alabama Civil Rights		
2	Brussels language riots		
3	Ulster religious feuds		
4			Indian refugees
5			Football fans
6	Grosvenor Square demonstrations		
7			Ku Klux Klan
8		Fiery cross on door	
9		Synagogue daubing	
10			Hitler arriving
11	Gas ovens at concentration camp		
12	Sharpeville		

* Including both fighting and scenes of dead or injured.

Table 3 shows that the dramatic structure of the edited film sequence moved from straight violence, through light relief to the tragic aftermath of violence. Table 3 also makes clear that the film sequence brought together a remarkable diversity of events and issues under the umbrella of 'prejudice'. The item showing demonstrations in Grosvenor Square was scripted as if to recognize the basic doubt surrounding the definition of prejudice:

But while some dance on the field, others demonstrate in the
street – though whether you call this prejudice or not rather
depends whether you are inside the American Embassy or outside.

(Programme I, final version)

The film sequence only achieved the full length (shown in
Table 3) as a result of continual attempts to obtain more
material from the film libraries. The director was insistent that
they should use more library film, because it had been included
in the budget. The producer agreed and left the director to find
more film. The director mentioned to the researcher that he
wanted to find illustrations of the pre-war Mosley rallies,
suffragettes, disturbances in Notting Hill and the Nazis. He
was aware that the producer had previously rejected Nazi film
as over-exposed, but he argued that Fascism was the prime example of prejudice in this century, and moreover such film was
easy to obtain. The director also suggested they should look
for something on Hippies and on the Mods and Rockers. The
conversation continued:

Researcher: What about students, CND and that sort of
thing?
Director: That's not really prejudice, is it?
Researcher: No, but they are in-groups and out-groups aren't
they? If you are going to have Hippies you could
have students.
Director: I suppose so if they were in a tightly identified
group.

This conversation shows again the ambiguity within the production team surrounding the concept of prejudice. Since her
earlier conversation with the producer mentioned above, the
researcher had adopted 'in-group/out-group' as her criterion of
prejudice. This conversation also shows why Nazi film clips
finally found their way into the programme. Fascism was a
dominant conventional symbol of prejudice and the film clips
were conveniently available.

THE INTERVIEW STATEMENTS AS TYPES OF KNOWLEDGE

There were six main themes on which the interviews were based: the producer outlined the four main themes on which the interviews were based and an analysis of the interview transcripts shows that two other themes had also been developed in the interviews:

1　The definition of prejudice.
2　The actual prejudices which individuals themselves held or admitted.
3　Statements relevant to the question, 'where does prejudice come from?'
4　Illustrations of different types of prejudice, including in-group/out-group relationships.
5　Statements relevant to the question how best to combat prejudice.
6　Statements relevant to the feelings which particular minority groups had for the majority or other minorities.

Table 4 shows the main types of interviewee who provided statements relevant to each theme. It also categorizes the different types of knowledge which were available under each heading from the different interviewees. The six interview themes can be subdivided into those which tapped the interviewee's own special experiences and those which asked for general opinions, such as might be held by any member of the general public. The categories used in Table 4 extend this division to show that the range of knowledge and opinion from which selection was made was limited both by what had been filmed, and the fact that many of the recorded interviews were not usable. The process of picking interview material can hardly be described as a selection process at all, since the problem was mainly to sort the usable from the useless.*

---

* 'Selection' implies picking from a large number of alternatives which for reasons explained were not available in this case.

TABLE 4

INTERVIEWEE STATUS AND TYPE OF KNOWLEDGE*

Theme No.	Theme	Type of interview	Type of knowledge
1	Define prejudice	Vox Pop	General opinion
		Individual interviewees	General opinion
2	Prejudices held	Vox Pop	Personal opinion
		Prejudiced (3)	Personal opinion
3	Where does prejudice come from	Experienced (3)	Professional experience
		Individual interviewees	General opinion
4	Illustrations of types of prejudice	Victims (10)	Personal experience
		Representatives (3)	Situation Report
		Research workers (2)	Research Report
5	Irradicating prejudice	Victims	General opinion
		Representatives	Situation Report
6	Feelings within minority groups	Victims	Personal experience
		Representatives	Situation Report
		Experienced	Professional experience

* This table summarizes the main types of interview and interviewee. There was some overlap in the questions asked of different interviewees. The terms used in the table are explained at length in the text.

General opinion refers mainly to opinions from the 'Vox Pop' interviews which were not based on any special knowledge or competence. *General opinion* definitions of prejudice were relatively difficult to extract. This question asked of the indivual interviewees tended to be much more productive than it was in the 'Vox Pops', presumably because prejudice was a more salient concept for the individual interviewees. Most of the people interviewed suddenly in the street did not attempt a definition. Those who did tended to give single words or short phrases, such as 'fear' or 'an inborn instinct'. One of the few who managed to give a more complex and coherent definition was a man wearing a clerical collar, for whom again prejudice was presumably a more salient and intelligible concept.

The attempt to use the 'Vox Pops' to make people admit to their own prejudices, an example of *Personal opinion*, was also largely unsuccessful. Most people felt they were not prejudiced.*

TABLE 5

TYPES OF PREJUDICE ADMITTED TO BY
'VOX POP' INTERVIEWS†

No, none	32	
Yes (unspecified)	5	
Against younger generation	1 ⎫	
Against coloured people	1 ⎪	
Against English Domination of Wales	1 ⎬ Total Specific Prejudices 4	
Against the Welsh	1 ⎭	

† This tabulation was made from the transcripts and does not include refusals to answer.

As shown in Table 5 only four specific, explicit statements of prejudice were secured through the 'Vox Pop' interviews.

Of the three *prejudiced* individual interviewees who also provided *personal opinion*, two were vicars and the third, much the most successful contact, was a lecturer in Social Psychology, James Mottram. He first came to the production team's notice because of a correspondence in the *Spectator*. He had criticized current plans for anti-discriminatory legislation and had in

* Other research using much more sophisticated techniques than the 'Vox Pops', has found it difficult to get people to admit that they, themselves, hold prejudiced opinions or engage in discriminatory acts. This apparently reflects the social climate current at that time, in which prejudice tended to be regarded as a pejorative term. See for example, Daniel, W. W., *Racial Discrimination in England*, Harmondsworth, Penguin, 1968.

turn been criticized for the racialist tenor of his views by other correspondents, including Professor Henri Tajfel. James Mottram was explicit and articulate about his views. In contrast one of the vicars was a religious fundamentalist whose prejudiced opinions were obscured behind biblical references and the other discussed the relationship between Christianity and other religions. Neither could be used generally as examples of prejudice in the series, although at one point the first vicar came close to saying that the Jews were guilty because of the murder of Christ. This passage was used in a later programme.

> ... the question is often answered (*sic*) are they, does any guilt apply to them today for rejecting Christ? And I would say 'No'. But I would say that they put the guilt on their descendants by saying his blood be upon us and upon our children, and of course they have had a very unfortunate history since then.
>
> (Interview transcript)

This passage illustrates the point that in normal speech most people do not use neat grammatical sentences. They tend to follow their train of thought as it leads them. This made it especially difficult to pick out the short coherent statements the producer wanted for these programmes. A viewer, seeing only a short selected piece had no 'run up' time to the sound of the person's voice and the idiosyncrasies of his manner of speaking. Thus, in the above quotation, the first sentence by itself did not make sense. If the producer had quoted these words on paper, it would have been legitimate for him to alter the first sentence to make grammatical sense with the rest of the passage. Because the words were spoken on film, however, they could not be tampered with. Film as a spoken medium is less flexible than film as a visual medium. This is one example of several items which had to be used even though they were less than perfect. Other items fell on the other side of this borderline. From the start of planning for *The Nature of Prejudice* a central idea for the series had been to record prejudiced statements on film or in the studio. In practice the few examples of actual prejudice available to the producer provide a good example of why 'selection' at this stage meant 'picking out the usable'.

The interviews with the *victims* of prejudice were more productive of statements about their *personal experience*, the third type of knowledge shown in Table 4. Of the sixteen interviews with *victims* of prejudice, six of these were not usable, because the interviewee did not manage to make a coherent statement to camera, or because the interviewee asserted discrimination without providing sufficient evidence. The producer's journalistic sense made him doubt the authenticity of such claims. Many of those who are *victims of prejudice*, and who belong to underprivileged minority groups, also lacked the verbal skills necessary to present their case clearly and concisely. Moreover, it is difficult to provide evidence in an interview. The interviews with the gypsy, the ex-prisoner and two of the coloured interviewees taxed them up to and beyond the limits of their verbal skills. A passage from the transcript of the interview with the gypsy illustrates the effect of both criteria, coherence and authenticity. In a face-to-face situation this would have been a graphic account of an eviction, but it was quite unsuitable for television use:

> . . . so the caravan went down in a pot hole in the lane and some object, I was in the water in a pool of water in the hole – went up and (. . .) onto the wheel of the caravan and (. . .) my little boy was asleep in the bunk and he fell off. One of the panel pins got him in the head. Now I told the policeman, the child is injured I want to take him to hospital (. . .) the child was very bad see followed me all along Dudley (. . .) pull in and pull out again. So the next morning I bring the child to the police station (. . .) and they told me to get out first, they told me to get out the police station first, alright (. . .) so the sergeant called me back and said what happened then so (. . .) emergency operation straight away and he was in the hospital for 7 weeks. I took him out that day and the day I took him out I had to bring him back that evening again to a different hospital in Wolverhampton where he had another emergency operation (. . .) injured (. . .) so when I got back to the

hospital then after leaving Johnnie I found out that my wife had given birth to a baby at half past eight.
(Interview transcript: sections in brackets could not be
transcribed.)

This passage includes one of three accusations about the behaviour of the police made by interviewees. A general complaint of prejudice and discrimination by a coloured interviewee was rejected completely for lack of authenticity. The third accusation occurred in the middle of a statement by one of two young men. This statement was used twice, but on both occasions the middle section, which contained the most serious allegations about police behaviour, was omitted. There was no corroborating evidence and if allegations of this sort were to be made on television, the producer felt he needed to be sure of his facts. There was little possibility in this case of proving facts in an interview.

Of the eight race and colour *victims* interviewed half were rejected for lack of coherence or authenticity. Of the four remaining only two interviewees were actually used to describe their own experiences of white racial or colour prejudice. One of these was a white foster mother who had fostered several coloured children, and the other was a leader of one of the West Indian organizations. The producer was particularly pleased with two other interviews which showed examples of racial prejudice between those who would normally only be considered as its victims.

The *experienced* interviewees, the two headmistresses and the social worker, were asked to comment on prejudice as they saw it affecting others. There is a narrow dividing line between their *professional experience* and the *situation reports* provided by leaders of organizations representing various minorities.* Both types of interviewee generally yielded more usable material than the three types discussed above. In both cases the interviewees were outside the group of people they represented and able to discuss the minority's situation in the third person. The

* Terms taken from Table 4 above, p. 75.

representatives in particular made coherent, extended statements with relatively little prompting from the producer as interviewer.

Table 6 shows that the three *representatives* were the most fruitful source of programme material. The sixteen *victims* averaged 2·2 usages per interviewee, while the three *representatives* were used a total of 14 times.* No *representatives* were rejected as unusable. Half the *representative* usages were devoted to the most proficient speaker of the three. But more important

TABLE 6

USAGE OF DIFFERENT CATEGORIES OF INTERVIEWEE†

Category of interviewee	No. of cases	Individual no. of usages	Total no. of usages	Average no. of usages
Victims	10	1:1:2:2:2:2:2:3:3:4	22	2·2
Prejudiced	2	1:4	5	—
Experienced	3	3:3:4	10	4·7
Research workers	2	1:4	5	—

† Usage was defined as each complete film appearance regardless of length.

than personal verbal facility was the fact that those with *representative* and *experienced* status were able to provide qualitatively different material. The *victim*, used most frequently in the programmes was the Secretary of the West Indian Standing Conference, so that he was also able to make statements about the general racial situation in much the same way as the *representatives*. The two *research workers*, who were able to provide *research reports* on their own work, were also asked to give their general opinion on other aspects of the subject. The one who was prepared to generalize about the racial situation in much the same way as the *representatives* and the *experienced*, was also the one used most frequently.

* This averages 4·7 usages per interviewee, but with so few cases the mean is liable to be misleading.

A tentative conclusion emerges from this analysis. Personal generalizations about third parties is the type of knowledge most likely to be conveyed through television.

OUTLINES AND SCRIPTS

In general the producer, writing the programme scripts, worked as a 'compiler', combining the various inputs into programme form. Apart from the outline for the Network Planning Committee, written on production day 2, the first programme outlines were prepared on production day 7 for Programmes I and II. These outlines were based on the instructions given for the researching stage and they incorporated the material already known to be available.

The first script version of Programme I, completed on day 22, started with various definitions of prejudice, examples of violent prejudice, the categories sociologists use to label different people's prejudices, and the prejudices to which people would admit. These were to be illustrated, respectively, by a 'Vox Pop' sequence, a newsreel film sequence, stills, and another 'Vox Pop' sequence. The second part of the script used individual interview statements to show that prejudice took unexpected forms. In the third section, interview statements raised the question, from where does prejudice come? Finally, a film sequence of children at play was designed to interest the audience in the next programme.

Initially only two types of usable interviewee were omitted from the first script version. These were the two *victims* of inter-generational prejudice and two *prejudiced* people. One of each of these was used in later versions of the scripts so that finally no type of interviewee was excluded. The producer could edit the filmed interviews as he wished, to contribute to the writing of the script, but looked at the other way round, this meant that the scripts had to be written to fit the limited range of material available in the interviews. Even though most of the film specially shot for *The Nature of Prejudice* was of 'talking heads', the fact that these talking heads were on film rather than in the studio meant the producer could exercise greater control over their use, to develop an argument in the script or to vary the pace of a programme.

The presenter's first link in the script version of Programme I followed the opening of 'Vox Pop' sequence in which different definitions of prejudice were put forward by members of the public. After posing the question 'How would you define prejudice?', the presenter went on to quote the dictionary definition and to enlarge on its inadequacies by stressing that prejudice was a mental attitude which found expression in discrimination and suffering for large groups of people. This was the nearest the production team themselves had come to a definition, nevertheless, in the script the definition was qualified with the phrase 'that is how the psychologists describe it'. A similar qualification was placed against the four 'sociological' categories which ranged from 'all weather liberals' to 'active bigots'. 'But although the sociologists have us so neatly docketed we find it more difficult to place ourselves on the scale'. The producer pointed out when the director questioned this classification system, that as they had been attributed to sociology, the programme itself need take no responsibility for their accuracy.* They were used in Programme I, because they showed the variety of prejudice, and could be illustrated by stills.

These categories were followed by the presenter confessing to his own prejudices. As a performer, the presenter had a public *persona* the programme could use. A series of historical examples of prejudice followed, selected by the producer. The third section of the script posed the alternatives of heredity or environment as causes of prejudice. Four individual interview statements were included, three of which were from the two headmistresses. One statement held that children lacked colour consciousness at school. The producer inserted a link after the

---

* The academic credentials of these categories were obscure even in the original adult education outlines. A similar classification may be found in Rose, P. I., *They and We*, New York, Random House, 1964.

first of the interview statements in which the presenter drew the conclusion that prejudice was not hereditary and asked again, where and how do children learn it? The answer, put forward in the three statements which followed, put the blame for the development of racial hostility on the parents. The presenter's closing remarks did not support or contradict this conclusion, but quoted the belief of an unnamed source 'that a bigoted person is well under way by the age of six – but by no means fully fashioned'.

Considerations of length made the producer transfer this final section from Programme I to Programme II. The first script for Programme II, prepared on day 30, began with the three statements that children learnt prejudice in the home, from their parents. Then the presenter questioned the parental theory critically. Two assertions in the presenter's link, that children become aware of racial differences very early and that children associate dirt and colour 'naturally', led up to the next interviewee statement. Both could be severely questioned. The first was inconsistent with Dr. Pushkin's findings and the second was not even consistent with one of the initial statements where it was claimed that children associate colour and dirt as a result of parental prompting, not 'naturally'.

The different use made of these statements in different contexts provides an extremely clear example of the interdependence between the producer's ideas and the material available to him. In general the scripts for the other programmes support this view of the producer as 'compiler' dependent on available inputs. An apparent exception, the later sections of the script for Programme II, is considered in detail in the following chapter.

CONCLUSION

The data presented in this chapter suggest some of the ways in which programme content is likely to emerge through the complex of factors involved in the television production process. Writing the programmes around available material underlines the importance of the contact mechanisms, discussed in the previous chapter. The subject and presentation chains which generated ideas about topics to cover, played less part in suggesting what should be said about them. The production team followed a variety of paths to collect material and subjected it to a variety of selection criteria, but these left little room for any concern about eventual meaning in the programmes. e.g. the interview material shifted from Programme I to II acquired a different meaning in the process. There was explicit ambivalence about the 'sociological' categories, implicit ambivalence about the presentation of the two research experiments. The archive film sequence was compiled mainly for visual effect, resulting in the inclusion of some odd activities as prejudice. Similarly, two examples of prejudice by coloured people were included to surprise the viewer without reference to the possibility that if he were white, the viewer might take this as a justification for his own attitudes.

Two generalizations may be drawn – on the one hand there was an unwillingness to commit the programmes to any particular view; on the other hand, views were allowed to emerge as a consequence of decisions influenced by presentation or audience attention. In the course of this study a distinction needs to be drawn between *communication*, attempts to transmit particular meanings to an audience, and *attention*, judging the level of audience satisfaction, keeping the viewer interested, and above all, making sure they do not switch off.* Various factors in television production seem to support an implicit philosophy that so long as the audience attends, communication can be left to take care of itself.

This chapter has also cast further light on the range of knowledge sampled through programme production. The selection criteria applied to the interview material favoured those in positions of leadership and responsibility as against those who simply had a personal experience to recount. General

* This distinction is similar to the distinction between *communication* and *satisfaction* discussed in Chapter I.

opinions were solicited even from those with specific expertise, apparently for fear that the detail might be boring and irrelevant and because opinions should always be balanced one against another. This reference to balance applies to the production team's general handling of all types of knowledge. The selection criteria used were based on legal, technological and audience factors. Some criteria, for example authenticity, had the negative effect of ruling out certain information and opinion. In sum, programme content was less a manifest consequence of decisions about its substance than a latent consequence of its passage through the production process itself.

5

The presenter and the studio guests *

SCRIPT REVISION

A 'positive' presenter had been chosen for the series, but it was unclear how far he could be expected or allowed to contribute to the series without encroaching on the producer's responsibilities. Initially, the producer accepted that the presenter would review the scripts to re-write his pieces into his own style. In practice the presenter went further. He suggested re-ordering of programme items and occasionally he made cuts in the substance of his links or he dropped a filmed interview statement in whole or in part. Less frequently, the presenter added an idea of his own. These different alterations involve something of a progression towards taking a producer-type role in relation to programme content. However, the revisions were completed quickly at a distance from the production team ensuring that the presenter worked within the framework of the material already prepared.†

There was little conflict between the producer and the presenter over these revisions. It was accepted that the presenter, appearing in public on the screen, would want to safeguard and develop a public *persona*. In one programme the presenter recounted his own prejudices, in another he used photographs taken at various stages of his career to make the point that,

* Outline summaries of the final programmes may be found in Appendix A.
† The producer's scripts were posted to the presenter who generally dictated his revisions to the p.a. over the telephone. The presenter only worked in company with the rest of the team on the recording dates.

during their life time, everyone belongs to a wide variety of social groups. Both these items were planned in early meetings between the producer and the presenter, to capitalize on the presenter's public *persona*.

The producer was also ready to accept the presenter's suggestions for script revisions simply because the presenter could give a 'second opinion'. The presenter was distanced from the programmes (he only worked with the production team on the recording dates), but he was himself highly experienced in television work. The presenter's distance helped him to 'take the role' of the viewer with the others in the team. Both initially in the script revisions, and later in planning discussions on the studio floor itself, he tended to base his arguments on his view of likely audience attention and reaction. Occasionally his suggestions would not work for visual reasons, or because the wording would not fit an interviewee's expression, and meaning.

The producer is responsible for hiring the presenter. The reputation of different presenters for interfering with the producer's ideas for programme content did influence the selection of the particular presenter for the series. Once selected, however, it is the presenter who will appear on the screen. In a case of real conflict he can do it 'his way' in front of camera, regardless of the producer's wishes. Producing a presenter is in many ways similar to producing any other performer. There was no such conflict between the producer and the presenter on *The Nature of Prejudice*. Nevertheless, it is clear that, in the short run, the producer has few sanctions and all of those which are available, such as editing the video-recording, are liable to involve heavy economic and professional costs for the producer himself. In the long run, he could 'spread the word' about the presenter's behaviour, but again this sanction is liable to be uncertain and may even rebound.

These general principles behind the process of script revision can be illustrated from the handling of Programme I. The presenter added one item and dropped another from the producer's script, but these were both changes in emphasis

D

more than substance, reflecting the presenter's responsibility for giving a second opinion on the coherence of programme items. The presenter also completely re-wrote all his linking pieces using his own phrases and occasionally his own illustrations to compress the expression. Here, as elsewhere, he was 'taking the role of the viewer', simplifying the content to the level he believed appropriate to the probable audience, by dropping or only alluding briefly, to some of the more complex points or obscure illustrations included in the producer's version.

The process of script revision was taken further as each programme reached the studio. The presenter and the production team met over lunch and then embarked on a series of rehearsals. These were necessary to coordinate the production technically and to show the production team how the programme material fitted together. Cuts had to be made on the studio floor to fit the programmes precisely into their time slot. The producer, presenter and director together decided what cuts to make, though the presenter, as the person actually appearing on the screen, generally carried his point with an argument based on his interpretation of viewers' interests and attention.

SELECTION OF STUDIO GUESTS

Studio guests were interviewed by the presenter in all the programmes of *The Nature of Prejudice* except the first. Programmes II–V in the series each divided into two sections, a sequence with the presenter linking filmed interview statements, followed by a discussion in the studio. Programmes VI and VII consisted entirely of studio discussions, but in Programme VI the guests were picked not for their expert status but to give examples of *prejudiced* opinion. These recordings were treated as equivalent to 'live' transmissions, so the producer could exercise much less control over the contributions of these studio guests than over the other types of programme input. After recordings it was possible to make small cuts – in fact for this series one programme was remade completely, another in part – but generally the producer and director hoped to get it right first time. Tampering with the video-recording was expensive, administratively inconvenient and liable to reflect adversely on their competence.

The studio guests were selected through the same mechanisms as those used to recruit the filmed interview subjects. The personal contact mechanism was particularly important in this case because the producer needed to judge each individual's likely capabilities in 'live' discussion. Of the eight experts used in the first five programmes, four were reached through mechanisms of personal contact, including the two social psychologists whose experiments had been filmed.

The producer wanted another psychologist, someone who was not well-known, to comment on these experiments. The researcher approached the Medical Research Council who suggested a well-known 'name'. The researcher reported this to the producer saying 'but he's a bit of a pundit isn't he?', a phrase suggesting both that this psychologist was well-known and over-exposed, and also that he was identified with a particular point of view in psychology. The producer also disagreed with this psychologist's approach. He suggested the researcher should try the Tavistock Institute. It took three more contacts with different organizations to reach a suitable social psychologist (Dr. J. Field). The difficulty experienced in recruiting Dr. Field confirms the obvious point that visibility is partly a result of past publicity. It also supports the arguments advanced above that personal contact mechanisms are liable to be the most effective.

Less than a fortnight before it was due to be recorded the producer decided to conclude Programme III (on 'in-groups and out-groups') with a studio discussion. Professor Hilde Himmelweit had previously been rejected as too over-exposed in the planning of guests for another programme but, on this occasion, shortage of time made the fact that she was visible and accessible a positive advantage. Finally, one guest expert, the lawyer Anthony Lester, was reached through the third contact mechanism, press reports. The planning of Programme V (on education or legislation to overcome prejudice) coincided with a well-publicized conference of the Campaign Against Racial Discrimination (C.A.R.D.) at which the white officers in the association, including Anthony Lester, had been replaced by coloured people.

The expert guests were recruited because of their specialized knowledge, but again their capabilities as 'studio material' and their visibility through the contact mechanisms appear to have been the most important factors in deciding which particular individuals were selected. In one case (Professor Jahoda in Programme V) the producer knew the expert had something special to say; in another he rejected a possible guest at least partly because he disagreed with his point of view. For Programme II the producer tried to prepare in detail what the guests would say but, in other cases, the guests were largely left to say what they thought was appropriate.

GUEST EXPERTS AND THE CONVERSATIONAL MODE (PROGRAMMES II–V)

The initial rough outline of Programme II based on the theme 'from where does prejudice come?', concluded with the following items:

(a) The question arises as to the psychological causes of prejudice. Is it due to repressive upbringing for instance? Is there such a thing as a prejudiced personality?
(b) The totalitarian personality.

The first version of Programme II included a complete script for the studio discussion starting with the presenter and Dr. Pushkin, whose experiment was shown in the programme, and then bringing in Dr. Field. According to this notional script the discussion was to include: a review of sampling procedures in social research; a discussion of the relationship between children's attitudes, the attitudes of their mothers and methods of child rearing, drawing on the theory of the *authoritarian personality*, and a discussion of the way prejudice is learned as part of the culture of a group. This last topic was to lead into 'in-groups and out-groups', the subject of the next programme.

At this stage the producer's plans were only tentative. He recognized that the 'live' studio discussions were to be conversations, not scripted recitations. Nevertheless, the producer did attempt to prepare the participants for this programme. He forwarded summaries of Dr. Pushkin's research to Dr. Field and to the presenter. Dr. Field returned his with a specific critique of the research and reported he was prepared to discuss the *authoritarian personality* and cultural influence. But, in spite of this planning, the studio discussion did not cover these topics.

Technical limitations in the studio were one reason for this. Comments from Dr. Field could not be included in the actual presentation of the research because there were too few studio cameras to cover every subject. But more important were the arguments advanced by the presenter at a meeting between all the participants immediately prior to the recording of the programme. The presenter was generally unhappy at the way the producer had attempted to give the discussion a notional script. He believed that discussion involving matters of opinion, rather than straight fact, were best done spontaneously, without rehearsal.

The discussion of the sampling method and that of the *authoritarian personality* theory were both dropped – the first because the presenter felt the public was now familiar with sampling through opinion polls, the second because he felt the theory was simply an academic complication.

Throughout this meeting the presenter adopted a form of argument which placed him outside the production team and linked him to the viewer. He described his own feelings watching the rehearsals as if he were simply a viewer, using such phrases as: 'What I and the viewer want to know is whether there is . . .'; 'What the viewer will want to see next is . . .'; or 'I think I would like to know next...'; 'I as a viewer would like to know...' He was able to adopt this form of argument because, compared to the others in the production team, he came to each programme fresh on the recording day and because he was actually appearing in the programmes. In most cases the producer was prepared to accept such arguments from the presenter.

The conversational mode used for the studio discussions hampered the presentation of the actual findings of the research in Programmes II and IV. As well as questioning the guests and drawing responses from them, the presenter summarized their statements in simple phrases and occasionally by illustrative analogies. Such simple phrases, produced spontaneously, were liable to distort the expert's meaning. For example, in Programme II Dr. Pushkin made two main statements summarizing his results. After the first the presenter concluded 'So they have in fact picked up their prejudices from their mothers'; after the second, 'So they did not pick it up from their mothers, they picked it up from their friends'.

Much less time was devoted to the exposition of Professor Tajfel's research in Programme IV. This was partly due to the doubts which the production team had about its validity and partly due to the lack of preparation for the later programmes, compared with Programme II. Professor Tajfel's results were left to emerge from the studio discussion but the brief conversation devoted to methods and findings never actually revealed what the experimental results were. After pushing Professor Tajfel twice towards the concrete findings, the presenter abandoned the attempt and introduced a conversational point of his own. Why, he inquired, had Professor Tajfel asked the children to say whether the men in the photographs were 'English' or 'not English', rather than 'British' or 'not British?' Was this prejudice against the Welsh or the Scots? This point appeared to be based on the presenter's own interest in Scottish nationalism.

After the presentation of results Dr. Field was brought into the discussion which moved towards more general topics. These general discussions illustrate another property of the conversational mode, the tendency to lay a variety of theories and explanations end to end without giving the viewer any means of judging between them. For example, in Programme II Dr. Field, after agreeing that children were likely to pick up prejudice from outside the home, moved on to consider the effect of Britain's imperial history on British racial attitudes. The presenter replied:

> But surely Dr. Field, I mean this is true, but surely a lot of people who hold colour prejudice aren't aware of this – they're not even educated people. Isn't the reason, I mean I don't know about this, I'm just having a guess, isn't the reason why we feel as we do, as a lot of these people do, about coloured people is because they're about as different from white people as you can get . . .

The presenter was here putting a point which he assumed would be in the minds of the viewers. It was a point to which he returned to continually in the course of the series so that *difference* became one of the most repeated explanations for racial attitudes, even though it was intended primarily as a conversational 'Aunt Sally'. The presenter took part in the discussions if not as an equal, at least as a conversational partner who could challenge the experts' opinions and occasionally assert one of his own. One of his objections to the thorough preparation of Programme II was that it robbed him of the opportunity to criticize Dr. Pushkin's use of the word 'hostility' to describe white children's attitudes to black.

After the experience of Programme II the producer made little attempt to prepare or rehearse the discussion for Programme III. The guest, Professor Himmelweit, viewed the first part of the programme during rehearsal with little knowledge of what it contained and few preconceptions as to what she should say. One of the *prejudiced* interviewees was featured prominently on film in Programme III. It was not clear to Professor Himmelweit that the production team were using his statements simply as examples of prejudiced opinions. As he was captioned 'Lecturer in Social Psychology', she devoted a good deal of attention during the discussion to demolishing his arguments as those of a fellow social psychologist. For the production team there was a clear difference between the roles of the studio guests and the filmed subjects. Whereas the team *used* the filmed statements, they were *dependent* on the studio guests. As a result they seemed to assume that viewers would take the guests' contributions as authoritative statements, while recognizing the special purposes for which the filmed statements had been included. In the case of Programme III the confusion was so great that the studio discussion was later completely remade, on the instigation of Professor Himmelweit. She felt that in rebutting the views of the other social psychologist, she had not done justice to the points raised by the presenter.

The same tendency was also implicit in the use made of the filmed interview statements. For example, Programme V discussed means of eradicating prejudice; statements from two coloured interviewees with opposing views were used to lead up to two studio discussions, one on education, the other on legislation. Anthony Lester, after he had been invited to discuss legislation on the programme, sent the producer some papers setting out his own views on the recent Racial Discrimination Act and containing his suggestions for further legislation. The *experts* in the other programmes had all been academics. They were all to an extent detached from the subject. The producer knew that all were likely to accept and support the generally 'liberal' position current in academia. He also knew that the views of the lecturer in Social Psychology who had been recorded on film were very atypical of those held by academics in general. But Anthony Lester was involved in the subject and had his own point of view which he wanted to assert.* Before the programme the producer and the presenter prepared to meet

---

* The production team occasionally recognized and rejected partisanship in academic terms too, as shown by the rejection of the eminent psychologist mentioned above with the phrase 'He's a bit of a pundit'.

and challenge this point of view. There was little need for this in the discussion. Anthony Lester presented all sides of the argument before stating his own views.

After Programme II the main residual form of content control was best demonstrated by the preparations made to counter Anthony Lester's points in Programme V. In this case the aim was not to make a particular point but to ensure that any points which were made, would be covered by contrasting alternatives. The conversational mode of discussion ensured this. So too did the recruitment of Dr. Field to take part in Programmes II and IV to challenge the findings of Dr. Pushkin and Professor Tajfel. But in both cases the conversational mode inhibited any exposition of their research results.

This account of the studio discussions includes a number of implicit hypotheses about audience reaction and understanding, some of which were investigated in the audience research carried out as part of this project and reported in Chapter 6.

THE SPECIAL CASE OF PROGRAMME VI

Programme VI departed from the format of earlier programmes in the series. The producer planned to use studio discussions as a vehicle through which to illustrate *prejudiced* opinion and examine *prejudiced* personalities. Programme VI was a special case because it was difficult to recruit such personalities using the contact mechanisms. As a result, the programme idea went through various changes and realizing the idea on the screen involved many additional problems, so that finally the programme had to be remade on the instigation of the executive producer. Programme VI was not planned until after studio work had started on the series, so the presenter was able to make more suggestions about the basic shape and content of this programme than any of the others. Also, because it was to be based on studio discussions, it was more dependent on his special expertise than the previous programmes. Programme VI began to take shape in discussions on the studio floor between the producer, presenter and director, following the recording of Programmes III and IV.

In these discussions guests were considered who would illustrate a variety of prejudices but who were visible to the production team in three different ways. An extreme Protestant and an extreme Roman Catholic, contracted at an early stage in planning for this programme, were examples of guests visible as members of organizations or social categories. A senior military officer and a retired Chief Constable were also considered as possible protagonists in a sequence illustrating inter-generational conflict, though these two were both considered as categories rather than individuals. No guests of this type were eventually used in either version of the programme. The religious spokesmen were rejected, on the insistence of the presenter, for fear that the discussion would become obscurely theological. Another problem was that having chosen a category, the producer still had to find an individual within the category who would express the views he wanted in a suitable form. The researcher had considerable difficulty contacting examples of prejudiced people on some of the topics suggested. As she put it, 'you get the impression there are lots of people shooting their heads off about mini skirts and that sort of thing, but when you come to look for them they are difficult to find. It's going to be difficult to find someone on women too – they don't join associations for that.'

Finding individuals from the two other sources available was easier. One group was more visible because they had already been contacted or interviewed in connection with earlier programmes in the series. Prominent among these was James Mottram, the lecturer in social psychology, whose *prejudices* had been quoted extensively on film in earlier programmes. When the presenter suggested he would need support to counter Mottram's apparent expertise, the producer suggested Peter Marsh, a sociologist, and one of the two *research workers* interviewed on film earlier in the production.

The general media culture was the third means through

which possible guests became visible to the production team. Various *public persons* prominent for the views they had expressed in various media were considered for a confrontation on the issue of inter-generational prejudice with one of the 'hairy' young men previously interviewed on film. Two ladies in the public eye were considered as possible opponents of an anti-feminist before Naomi Lethbridge was finally selected to confront Sir Cyril Osborne, himself a prominent public figure, well known through media appearances.

The final plan for the first version of Programme VI was to hold three confrontations; between James Mottram and Peter Marsh on racial attitudes; between Sir Cyril Osborne and Naomi Lethbridge on anti-feminism; and between Auberon Waugh and Mike Fearen on the inter-generational issue. Thus, half of the guests for the first version of the programme were people who had appeared on film in earlier programmes. The other half were drawn from the general media culture.

These confrontations were planned with the expectation that the *prejudiced* participants would reveal themselves for what they were and that the other participants, with the support of the presenter, would at least be able to hold their own. In practice, this expectation was not realized. Peter Marsh treated James Mottram too politely to counter the latter's arguments effectively. Sir Cyril Osborne was not keen to talk on the subject of women at all in case it damaged his political image. He was angry at being deprived of a platform for his views on immigration, the subject on which he thought he had been asked to speak. Auberon Waugh treated Mike Fearen very reasonably, taking the line that though he did not like his appearance, he did not see how he could object to someone else's tastes.

Usually, after the recording of a programme, the executive producer rang through to say he liked it and to offer a few comments or criticisms. After this recording there was no telephone call, but next morning the executive producer called in the director and later the producer to tell them that, in his opinion, the programme 'did not add up to anything'. If the aim had been to show portraits of three bigots, this should have come over very powerfully, but in practice the confrontations had all misfired. The executive producer also criticized the presenter for handling the programme in a very old-fashioned way. As the presenter was not present at this discussion, there was perhaps a tendency to account for the failure of the programme by picking on the way he had conducted the confrontations. The producer felt that the presenter had intervened too much. But, as the executive producer pointed out, in deciding to hire this presenter they had opted for one who had himself something to contribute and who was not simply a vehicle for charm. The executive producer had no doubt that the programme should be remade, and, once they had discussed its faults the other two agreed. The question then was how to avoid a repetition of the previous failure.

By this time the researcher had left the production team so that the producer and director had, themselves, to come up with ideas for people to interview. At this point the producer thought about abandoning Programme VI altogether and just turning in a six-programme series, but both realized that no-one would be pleased with that, least of all the budget and presentation departments. The producer was inclined to use some of the people they had already had on the series, especially James Mottram – 'he gives doesn't he?' – but the executive producer countered that he was not important. *Importance* was another characteristic of those visible through the general media culture. Sir Cyril Osborne for example was *important* both because he was a well-known public figure and because he was connected to centres of power in society through his position as Conservative Member of Parliament. But *importance* also had other meanings. At a later stage the executive producer suggested that Roy Sawh, one of the Black Power spokesmen, would be better than James Mottram, because he was more *important* (significant) in terms of current social developments. On another occasion however the presenter argued strongly for the *importance* of Mottram, as someone who would express views widely held in

Britain, which would be recognized by many viewers as their own.

As they considered how to remake the programme, the production team were thrown back on following the various models available from other television programmes shown in the past and to drawing their interviewees from available members of the general media culture. The executive producer for example suggested that if they were planning to present three *prejudiced* personalities, they should have a psychiatrist in the studio to give an analysis of each individual after he had spoken. He pointed out that for the BBC series *Face to Face*, the presenter's questions had been carefully prepared with expert psychiatric advice. The producer, however, felt that three people 'in the public eye', would not care for a public psychoanalysis session. The executive producer was worried how the presenter alone would be able to bring out the meaning of the three interviews. The producer suggested using the four categories, included in Programme I, so that at the end the presenter could say 'I think these people are x, y and z, but then I'm probably w, what do you (the viewer) think you are?' This idea was developed in discussion until, finally, a plan was evolved to show a potted biography of each of the three people at the end of the programme and then assign them to a particular category. The production team had expressed doubts about the worth of these 'sociological' categories when they had included them in Programme I. On this occasion they fitted the format planned for the programme, but the idea lapsed because both the director and the p.a., who had to make the technical arrangements, distrusted the categories.

Replanning Programme VI took several days in the course of which the producer reformulated the basic idea of the programme. It was to show *prejudice*, but also to show that *prejudice* was 'two sides of the same penny'. Where the viewer recognized prejudice would depend on his own views. The programme could be introduced like this so as to avoid antagonizing the guests.

The producer and director considered illustrating a variety of prejudices: anti-Semitism, anti-feminism, religion, Scottish or Welsh nationalism, social snobbery – but each was rejected for want of someone who would really 'come across' on any of these subjects. Various public figures who were generally identified with a right-wing position, such as Robert Pitman and Kingsley Amis, were considered before the producer hit on one, Lady Dartmouth, who was well-known for making rigid statements about Hippies, sex and pornography; and another, Peregrine Worsthorne, who was a staunch Roman Catholic as well as a defender of traditional élitism in British society. James Mottram was retained as the third interviewee. To handle these interviews alone the presenter needed to prepare his hand; the director arranged for another researcher to brief the presenter with some of the published views of Lady Dartmouth and Peregrine Worsthorne.

Special problems were also involved in realizing Programme VI on the screen. The presenter introduced the programme to the viewer with the following statement outlining the purpose of the programme:

> Up to now in this series we have looked at prejudice through the eyes of the sociologist and the social psychologist, the educationist and the lawyer. We have interviewed victims of prejudice. But today I want to discuss the subject with three intelligent people – all three of whom have strong views on a wide variety of subjects. I think I should probably describe them as prejudiced persons. They may well return the compliment. It will be up to you as viewers to judge between us. Whether your judgement is impartial or not will probably depend on the kind of prejudices you yourselves have.

This opening statement was one attempt to redefine the studio interviews in this programme as exposures of *prejudiced* personalities rather than conversations with experts, such as had been seen in earlier programmes. The production team had tempered the opening statement because the three guests were sitting in the studio waiting to be interviewed. (As one member of the production team put it, 'we don't want them walking off the set at the last moment'.) However, captions were used to identify the three guests, which gave not only their names but also their occupation. These suggested that the interviewees had the same claim to 'expert status' as the guests who had appeared in earlier programmes. And to some extent this was supported by the way the presenter handled the interviews.

The first interview with James Mottram was characterized by an aggressive battery of short-fire questions and interruptions, which made Mottram appear as if he were 'in the dock', called upon to answer charges against him. It opened with a clip from the earlier filmed interview in which Mottram commented that coloured people were not particular about the cleanliness of their environments, that they were socially and psychologically incompatible with British society, and that 'we should be considering civilized ways of sending them home'. After giving Mottram an opportunity to retract, the presenter asked him whether he had an obsessional dislike of coloured people. Mottram denied this and then referred to the way he had redefined prejudice in an earlier programme. The presenter went on to ask Mottram whether he felt afraid of coloured people or superior to them. In the course of this discussion Mottram quoted the views of various academic authorities. The presenter countered with a reference to a study by the United Nations, but he was unable to quote the findings in detail when Mottram questioned the methodology. Eventually, Mottram agreed that he accepted the views of 'geneticists' who held that coloured people were inferior to white people in various ways. The presenter accused him of 'talking in a way that Hitler used to talk about the Jews'. Mottram retorted that that was unfair, that evident truths stated in sober scientific language were not offensive. Hitler, he claimed, had not defined his terms in a scientifically acceptable way.

This confrontation shows some of the problems involved in realizing the programme idea. By referring to academic authorities and to his own appearance on a previous programme

James Mottram continued to appear as an academic expert, similar to those who had been seen in earlier programmes. The presenter was forced to cite an alternative academic authority to counter Mottram's argument, but without the necessary knowledge to back it up. Then he resorted to an appeal to cultural symbolism with the reference to Hitler.

The other two guests were both known personally to the presenter. They were *public persons* from the same media culture as the production team. Whereas the presenter was strongly opposed to the views expressed by Mottram, he seemed to regard the views of the other two as less serious eccentricities. In the interview with Lady Dartmouth, the presenter modified his inquisitorial technique using a more conversational approach. He was more careful and apologetic about interruptions. The third interview, with Peregrine Worsthorne, appeared even more amiable, a discussion between two men on some points about which they disagreed.

The fact that the presenter interrupted James Mottram sixteen times, more than twice as often as either Lady Dartmouth or Peregrine Worsthorne, provides one numerical index of these differences in treatment. Another was that although each interview was roughly equal in length, Mottram made twice as many statements as the other two interviewees. On average each of his statements was half as long as those of the other two. There was also variation in the way the three interviews were shot. Extremely large facial close-ups, designed in some way to show the subject for what he or she really was, were used extensively in the first two interviews, taking up nearly 40% of the time. The 'full face' shot was not used at all in the last interview. In combination, these measures of programme content suggest that the production team were demonstrating that James Mottram was outside their own world, both socially and in terms of his views.

Once again this account involves implicit hypotheses about likely audience reaction. The audience study, reported in Chapter 6, makes it clear that many viewers accepted the

opinions of the *prejudiced* guests, especially when they
with their own, and thought that these guests were also

GLOBAL THINKERS—PROGRAMME VII

Once the executive producer had become involved in the remaking of Programme VI, he also asked questions about the
plans for Programme VII. From the first this had been designed
as a conclusion to the series in which definitions and general
ideas on prejudice would be discussed by a studio panel. A
number of people in public and academic life were considered
for inclusion in this panel before the producer decided on the
six listed below.

FIRST STUDIO PANEL FOR PROGRAMME VII

	Main reason for selection
Professor Harry Street	Authorship of *Street Report* on Legislation and Racial Discrimination.
Dr. Dypak Nandy	Known interest in problem through personal contact and previous television appearances.
Mark Bonham Carter	Chairman of the Race Relations Board.
Timothy Raison	A neutral, rational Conservative, 'outsider'.
Dr. J. Field	Contracted as psychologist for earlier programmes. Known interest in subject.
Professor Henri Tajfel	Contracted to demonstrate research in earlier programmes. Known interest in subject.

These guests were chosen because they were visible, available
and known to be interested in the subject; not because they
were known to have anything special to say. After the first
recording of Programme VI the executive producer commented
that too many guests of the wrong type had been selected. He
argued that they should find *global thinkers*, people able to
analyse the problem in a wide historical context. His initial

example of a *global thinker* was Edmund Leach who had recently completed a series of controversial Reith Lectures. Edmund Leach was unable to accept an invitation to appear in Programme VII. He had been flooded with similar invitations after the Reith Lectures, suggesting that other production personnel worked in much the same way as those on *The Nature of Prejudice*. Various other candidates were considered as possible *global thinkers*. Professor A. J. Ayer was picked after he had been brought to the production team's attention by an article in the *TV Times*, which had accompanied the billing for the first programme in the series. The producer was anxious to include Mark Bonham Carter because, as the then Chairman of the Race Relations Board, he was involved with the problem in practice. The executive producer accepted him, saying 'Yes, he's on their level isn't he?', but he was less sure about Professor Tajfel, whom the producer had chosen to give a preliminary psychological definition of the word *prejudice*. A compromise was agreed whereby this definition sequence was to be kept separate at the start of the main programme.

Various formats for the programme were considered, modelled on three other programmes – *The Brains Trust*, *Panorama* and *Late Night Line Up*, all of which had used different panel discussion techniques. Stress was laid on the viewers' need to feel involved in the conversation. The executive producer argued that this would be helped if the discussion was conducted through the presenter. In this case the production team assigned to the presenter the role of viewers' representative, a role which he generally adopted for himself.

At the end of the planning period a third *global thinker* was still not available, so the producer decided simply to bring Professor Tajfel into the general discussion. This made the director, who was already worried about the practical difficulties of bringing such a studio discussion alive, even more apprehensive about the likely success of the programme. *Global thinkers* were renowned for being temperamental. The director was afraid that they would show their boredom and withdraw if they felt the discussion was beneath them. In practice the director's fears were not realized and Professor Tajfel took a leading part in the discussion. Nevertheless, his general thesis that *global thinkers* were liable to behave rather like *prima donnas* was supported by the temperamental behaviour which followed a mix-up over transport.

CONCLUSION

This discussion of the different studio guests may be linked to the earlier account of the selection of subjects for the filmed interviews. Some types of people are more visible to television than others and different people are liable to be put to different uses in the medium. The diagram on page 106 sets out a general schema ranging from the *ordinary citizen*, invisible to the medium and little used by it, to the *media stars*. Television selects those who will be presented according to the structure of power, authority and knowledge existing in society, but through the development of a media culture, it also super-imposes a structure of its own.

The *global thinkers*, a term used by the production personnel themselves, differed from the other guest experts in a number of ways. The experts who appeared in Programmes II–V were known to have some special interest or qualification for talking on a specific subject. The guest expert was expected to provide authoritative statements on a limited subject.

The *global thinkers* had achieved expert eminence in at least one field. But in their case it was accepted that their conver-sational competence extended beyond this particular field, so that they could provide worthwhile opinions whatever the topic. The continuous media exposure which was necessary for them to be recognized as *global thinkers*, was also thought to give them quasi-star status with the viewers. Two of the ex-amples of *prejudiced people* in Programme VI were public figures, known for their particular views. Unlike the *global thinkers* they were not expected to make authoritative state-

THE VISIBILITY AND USE OF DIFFERENT TYPES OF PEOPLE IN TELEVISION

Type of person	Unknown 'ordinary citizen'	Expert in special field / Spokesman of group or organization	Known expert in professional field / Spokesman or person in power position of minor importance / Media 'professional'	Accepted speaker on fields other than his own / Power figures of major 'importance' / Media 'stars'
Probable main use	'Vox Pops' and Studio audience / Filmed interview statements / —	— / Filmed interview statements / Studio guests Specific subject	— / — / Studio guests Specific and general subjects	— / — / Studio guests General subjects
Visibility to production team	Unknown / — / —	Contact mechanisms / — / —	Contact mechanisms / Media exposure / —	Media exposure / General culture / —
Frequency of use	Low			High

ments, although they shared with them the attribute of quasi-star status.

Different members of *The Nature of Prejudice* production team varied in the extent to which they preferred one type of guest to another. The executive producer, for example, was particularly keen on guests who were publicly well-known; i.e. the *global thinkers* and the public personalities. There were also differences in the relationship between members of the production team and the studio guests, depending on their status. The experts who appeared in most of the programmes, were referred to as 'guests on our programme'. There was resentment on the few occasions when these guests appeared about to upset programme plans, for example, by arriving late at the studio. On the other hand, there was much greater tolerance of the signs of temperament shown by some of the guests in Programmes VI and VII. It was accepted, even expected, that those who had achieved something approaching star status would demand special treatment. There was considerable hostility to James Mottram, however, when he appeared to be acting 'as if he was the star of the show' on the third occasion on which he travelled to London to appear in the series. The production team thought of James Mottram as their own discovery, even though that discovery had originally been made through the columns of a weekly journal. Nevertheless, he stands out as an exception to the general rule that the media tend to feed on themselves, in the people they present, as much as in the opinions they retail.

6*

The audience and the nature of prejudice

The 'success' of a television programme can be measured in many different ways. It is often said that both the BBC and the ITV programme companies tend to measure success by the size of the audience, but there are still programmes with a deliberately specialist appeal, to which different criteria may be applied. The exploratory audience research reported here looks at the success of these programmes against the background of the production process described in preceding chapters. In analysing the data available the main interest lay in trying to see whether and to what extent the audience saw the programme in the way the production team intended, and whether they reacted in the ways expected.

In order to study how the seven *Nature of Prejudice* programmes worked as communications, the same panel of adult and adolescent viewers were asked to fill in questionnaires after seeing each programme. Only a few individuals managed to see all the programmes. Even so, enough questionnaires were collected to allow some suggestions to be made about *characteristic* ways in which each programme in the series was perceived. It is doubtful whether the sample is representative of *all* the people who actually saw *The Nature of Prejudice* or to the much larger group of people in the country who might have seen the programme, but did not. But those who agreed to take part in this

* This chapter was written by Roger L. Brown who conducted the audience survey.

audience research did so voluntarily. One might expect their reactions to be more favourable than those of the people who, though asked, declined to take part in the research. In addition, the panel selected was on the whole middle class and fairly highly educated. On the basis of other research this would lead one to expect a lower incidence of negative and prejudiced reactions than might be the case with other sections of the public. All these factors tend to make some of the audience research findings appear surprising.

The number of completed questionnaires returned varied from a low of 131 for Programme IV to a high of 182 for Programme II. Altogether over 1,000 questionnaires were available for analysis. The ten or more questions asked about viewers' reactions to each programme yielded far more data than can be usefully summarized here. What follows are a number of *illustrations* of viewers' responses rather than an exhaustive treatment of the immediate effects of *The Nature of Prejudice*. These examples pinpoint a number of crucial ways in which the communicative success of a series can be judged. A useful starting point is to ask whether the viewers *understood* the programmes, before moving on to more evaluative and complex reactions.

During Programme I of *The Nature of Prejudice*, the phrase 'discrimination depends on identification' was used. This phrase formed a key part of the argument so the members of the viewing panel were asked to explain it. Only 31 (24%) of the 129 people who completed the question gave (loosely) correct definitions. Similarly, in the third programme, a key distinction was made between the terms 'assimilation' and 'integration'. 83 (67%) of the 123 panel members appeared to have grasped the essence of the difference. The arguments underlying these semantic distinctions may well have got across to some extent, but the figures suggest that abstract words can cause difficulties, even with relatively well educated audiences. It has often been argued that television is bad at putting over such abstract terms and arguments. Because they cannot be made visual, they are not elaborated sufficiently. The vocabulary of the general television audience is considerably more restricted than many television producers might imagine.

Programme II provided an opportunity for looking at a rather more demanding sort of 'comprehension'. In this programme, Dr. Pushkin demonstrated a series of three experiments examining manifestations of prejudice in white children. The research compared the frequency of prejudice among children in three areas of London. From the viewers' responses, however, one could not be sure what conclusion should be drawn from the comparison of the three areas. One group of viewers apparently believed that there were noticeable differences between the areas. However, a second, smaller group of viewers appeared to have seen the results from the three areas as the same or similar. There is no clear suggestion in the questionnaires that these two rather differing emphases had any connection with viewers' own prejudices or with any other factor. However, they serve to show how a rather *complex* communication may lend itself to different interpretations. Several of the main points of Dr. Pushkin's presentation came over to the audience clearly enough: the fact, for example, that prejudice is widespread and readily detectable at an early age, that it appears to rise to a peak at 6 years and then decline, and that parents play a very important part in the learning of prejudices. Perhaps one should add to this list the fact that although three areas were being compared, the result of the comparison remained ambiguous.

The experiment demonstrated by Dr. Tajfel in the fourth programme also led to a number of different responses on the part of viewers. Respondents were asked 'How would you yourself describe the results of one of Dr. Henri Tajfel's experiments with children?' This was itself an ambiguous question, inviting either an evaluative reaction or a more *descriptive* one. This ambiguity proved fruitful from the research point of view. Of the 130 viewers who provided completed questionnaires, only 36 (27%) offered a description of the results of the experiment.

These descriptions of the findings naturally varied considerably in explicitness and comprehension, but in many cases one wonders whether the sense made of Dr. Tajfel's work was what was intended. For example, one adult panel member wrote: 'That children stereotype adults on the basis of previous experience, e.g. a pleasant face, someone who is kind – an unpleasant face, someone who is not so nice.' The main point of persons being evaluated on the basis of the *categories* to which they have been allocated has been missed. Another who missed the point of the research thought the main finding was that 'Children, as well as adults, dislike people, unknown to them, on sight.' Another adult panel member wrote, 'I think the result of the experiment in sorting faces into English or non-English, by children age 6 to 11, shows that stereotypes have not yet been formed at that age. Another result is that children appear to like or dislike faces according to the characteristics of the face rather than the race,' an interpretation of the research findings which was directly opposite to that of the experimenter himself. There were viewers who saw the point of the research and said so, but there was a good deal of confusion and misunderstanding.

The reason for this confusion seems clear enough, both from a study of the programme content and from the questionnaire responses. The results were never stated. How this came about has been made clear in Chapters 4 and 5, 40 (31%) of the 130 panel members said that they hadn't noticed any 'results' being given. Quite commonly a wistful tone of voice crept into these answers. 'I wish I could. My main impression was that we were not given experimental results. Just a general hint that children make assessments of "strangers" early in life. We could have done with more tabulated results here.' Others (21% of the viewers) were more blunt, saying that they hadn't been told the results of Dr. Tajfel's work, and that the findings were 'Inconclusive', 'Unconvincing', 'Not impressive', or 'Not very conclusive'. Two adult panel members made specific reference to the presenter's apparent interruption of Dr. Tajfel just as he was getting to the point of summarizing what he had found out.

The annoyance caused to viewers by not being given the research findings may have been partly responsible for the number of references made to weaknesses in the research techniques themselves. Twenty-one (36%) of the 59 adolescents completing questionnaires commented on this feature of the presentation, though only six (8%) of the 71 adults did so. Perhaps we might expect sixth-formers to be more sensitive to this sort of thing. For example, one sixth-former commented, 'I have one criticism about this experiment and that is the little girl could not reach the "like" boxes very well, and might therefore have put the photographs in the "dislike" boxes because of this reason.' One viewer who apologized for not hearing the results of the experiment, went on to say that 'it appeared that the children shown did not know what they were doing and just placed the picture in the box they fancied'. A number of viewers thought that the task was too difficult for the children. 'Despite Dr. Tajfel's claims', wrote one viewer, 'I feel that the difficulty in separating the photos is tremendous, and the margin of error would be too great to draw any concrete conclusions.' The apparent *reason* for these comments was that viewers did not appreciate that what they saw was merely an approximate studio *simulation* of what Dr. Tajfel had actually done in his research. Since people are ready enough to be critical of social research it seems that either a better simulation was needed, or a much stronger statement that what was shown was intended merely as a rough illustration. It seems clear enough that the number of viewers who found the research as reported 'inconclusive' did so in this instance because the findings were not presented. It is worth suggesting that it may be very important to make the results of empirical research 'stick' in the viewer's mind in a series such as this which relies so heavily on the general perspectives of the social sciences. Badly presented results may well lessen people's faith in social research in general.

Of course, members of a television audience may understand

well enough what is actually said, but misperceive the basic underlying messages. The *manifest* content comes over clearly enough, but the *latent* content is distorted. Chapter 5 indicated that James Mottram was selected to appear in the sixth programme as an example of a prejudiced person. However, it is clear that a number of viewers did not perceive him as such. Panel members who saw the sixth programme were asked to note down remarks made by the guest speakers which they, the viewers, regarded as examples of prejudice. Of the 171 panel members for Programme VI, 22 (13%) did *not* cite one of Mottram's remarks as an example of prejudice. Some went further than this, indicating that they found Mottram a fully sympathetic figure. For example, one agreed with 'everything James Mottram said'; and another found him 'rational, fair and unbiased'; a third wrote: 'I felt I could agree whole-heartedly with the majority of James Mottram's remarks'. When viewers were asked to note down the two speakers they regarded as most prejudiced, 96 (56%) mentioned Lady Dartmouth first, whereas only 50 (20%) mentioned Mottram first. (Peregrine Worsthorne was mentioned first by only 15 (9%) of the panel.) Attempts to label Mottram as a prejudiced individual did not meet with unqualified success, but we shall have more to say about Programme VI later.

We all know that a group of people watching the same television programme can react to it in very different ways, even disagreeing about what it is 'saying'. Such an expectation was certainly borne out by *The Nature of Prejudice*. The questionnaires about the third programme in the series asked viewers to say what was the *main* point which the programme had been making about prejudice. In a half-hour programme a great deal happens, but even so, the range of answers was striking. One viewer gave a very general answer, one which might have applied almost equally well to any programme in the series, 'the main point about prejudice in the programme was the cause of prejudice and why people have prejudices against another group of people'. Several statements referred to the origins of prejudice, for example, 'Prejudice begins in the animal world, and exists among the lower forms of life'. Another viewer gave a less precise response that seemed to assume an 'instinct' theory: 'Prejudice is something ingrown, and could be quite natural'. One viewer referred to out-group characteristics: 'Colour plays a large part in prejudice, but different social customs and modes of conduct may also inspire prejudice.' Another viewer said that 'prejudice is largely the result of fear and ignorance'; another, 'that prejudice is an outlet for feelings of inadequacy, and is necessary'. Finally, one viewer noted the consequences rather than its causes, suggesting that 'prejudice nearly always leads to persecution'. These seven statements about the main point of Programme III show the variety of response.

But why do people vary so widely in what they make of the same television material? What viewers make of a particular programme results from the programme itself, and from what the viewer himself brings to the viewing situation in the way of knowledge, attitudes, expectations, likes and prejudices. Reactions are a composite of what the programme itself was saying and what the audience, in a broad sense, expected it to say.

The first programme in the series was in part designed to show the wide range of prejudices currently to be found in Britain, and perhaps by so doing to raise in viewers' minds a question about what is common to all these varied types of antipathy. A wide range of prejudices was mentioned in the programme, including prejudices against women, Jews, gypsies, homosexuals and lesbians, and against Hippies, but one type of prejudice – that against coloured people – predominated.

It is doubtful whether this could be demonstrated by a straightforward frequency count of the visual and verbal content of the programme, but it can perhaps be seen to emerge from the way anti-coloured prejudice 'slipped in' as an illustrative example at two separate points in the commentary. The explanation of the idea that 'discrimination depends on identification', for example, used the word 'colour(ed)' three times. The commentary ran as follows:

> Discrimination depends on identification. By seeing the colour of a man's skin or the pattern of his clothes, by recognizing his background, by the sound of his voice. A coloured man may disguise his accent when applying for a job over the telephone. The job, he hears, is open, yet when he applies, it has mysteriously been filled – and it's not only coloured people who get this kind of treatment.

Leading up to a question about the origins of prejudice in children at the end of the programme, the commentary again employed colour prejudice as an example: 'What causes prejudice, what makes one man a nigger hater, what makes another a nigger lover and a third don't know?' But unconscious attention given to colour in the spoken commentary is probably not sufficient in itself to explain the relative prominence it achieved as perceived by the viewers.

Members of the panel were invited to write down the two sorts of prejudice to which they thought Programme I had paid most attention. In all, 312 separate responses were given to this question. Of these the largest number, 81 (26%), involved references to racial prejudice, and a further 75 (24%) references to colour prejudice. There were only 41 (13%) mentions of religious prejudice, and 28 (9%) of anti-Semitic prejudice. Moreover, racial prejudice was mentioned first 69 times, but second only 12 times; colour prejudice was mentioned first 62 times and second only 13 times. Conversely, religious prejudice was only given twice as a first response, but 39 times as a second answer (the comparable numbers for anti-Semitic prejudice were 7 and 21). These figures suggest that viewers saw in the programme predominantly the type of prejudice – colour prejudice – which was most familiar and salient for them, and for contemporary British society at large. Prejudice today tends to *mean* colour prejudice. The audience members showed this clearly enough and in earlier chapters we have seen that the same may be said of the programmes' producers.

Little background data was collected about the members of the viewing panel, but it was possible to study differences between adult and adolescent viewers. As we have seen, the first programme set out to show that prejudices may be directed against a very wide range of different groups. Viewers were asked to write down any unfamiliar prejudice mentioned in the programme. In general, the younger viewers were more likely to mention a prejudice as unfamiliar (most frequently these would be prejudices against women and against sexual deviants). Older people have had many more opportunities of observing or hearing about various kinds of prejudice than younger people (though for this very reason they *might* have been less ready to admit ignorance). Panel members were also asked to say which sort of prejudice they thought Programme I paid most attention to, and here again there were some differences between age groups. More adolescents than adults mentioned racial prejudice, conversely more adults than adolescents, anti-Semitic prejudice. (These differences are harder to interpret. It may be that the adult viewers were more racially prejudiced than the adolescents, but wished to suppress this fact.)

There were also differences in the way younger and older viewers reacted to Programme VI. All but two (96%) of the 52 adolescents said that James Mottram was a prejudiced person, but only 63 (63%) of the 104 adults made this identification. (This is one of the reasons for thinking that the adults were more prejudiced than the younger people.) Similarly, whereas *all* the adolescents saw Lady Dartmouth as prejudiced, 16 adults (16%) did *not* see her as prejudiced. More of the older panel members (47% as against 23%) thought Peregrine Worsthorne prejudiced. Presumably Lady Dartmouth appeared prejudiced to the adolescents because she expressed views on the generation to which younger panel members themselves belonged.

Seeing *themselves* as the target of prejudice had another interesting effect on younger viewers. After seeing the first programme, viewers were asked to note down which characteristics of an out-group were most likely to lead to prejudice being directed *against* that out-group. It seems from the answers given that younger viewers sought to avoid terms of disapproval which are commonly applied to members of their own age group: 'long hair', 'strange clothes' or 'untidiness'. Only two (4%) of the adolescents used terms such as these compared to 26 (26%) of the adults. The younger viewers were more likely to use neutral terms like 'easy identification'.

We should not be too surprised that after seeing Programme II as many as 57 (73%) of the 78 adolescents 'blamed' prejudice on parents or the home background, while only 53 (53%) of the 104 adults did so. But there was a similar difference in identifying friends as a source of prejudice. Twenty-two (28%) of the 78 adolescents mentioned this, but only 15 (15%) of the 104 adults. Perhaps the importance of the teenage peer group lies behind this difference. The younger viewers were also more likely than adults to attribute prejudiced views to the mass media themselves and to other impersonal agents: One factor, more salient for the adults than the teenagers, was the colonial history of Britain: only 21 (27%) of the 78 teenagers mentioned this, against 57 (57%) of the 104 adults. While older people had lived through the dismantling of the colonial empire, younger people have merely come to learn of this as a part of history. All these differences tend to indicate how the real-life experiences of viewers markedly affect which aspects of television programmes are best remembered. Crudely put, what sticks in the mind is what one already, to some extent, knows.

The Nature of Prejudice was not really designed to change people's minds, but even so it seems clear that an understanding of viewers' reactions will be less than complete unless it is looked at in this light. The dividing lines between information, education and persuasion are always difficult to draw. Ever since the power of the mass media was demonstrated in fields such as advertising and political propaganda, people have looked to these media to solve or ease social problems, in particular by changing attitudes to foreign or minority groups. Experience from both World Wars seemed to suggest that it was possible to stir up dislike and hatred of the peoples of other countries: surely it should be possible to produce the opposite effect equally easily, and promote good relations between different groups? Unfortunately, these hopes have not been borne out by events, and there are sound reasons, as well as some supporting evidence, why they should not have been.

Many people believe that, since advertising seems to 'work', other kinds of persuasive communication ought to be just as effective. But advertising is a special type of communication. The lessons it teaches are not necessarily valid for other situations. In the first place, we *have* to buy food and soap, so the major decision is made before consumer advertising gets to work at all. Purchasing Brand X rather than Brand Y does not usually represent any basic change in our view of the world. The way that political parties advertise their leaders and policies is often compared to consumer advertising these days, but from the public's point of view deciding for a particular party is very different from deciding to buy Brand X. Attitudes to a political party are connected to a whole range of other attitudes and beliefs about social class, money, leadership, right and wrong, and possibly religion as well. For most people in a country like Britain, political choices are far more *central* than choices between brands. From the point of view of persuasive communication, it is really far harder to change our political beliefs (and our voting intentions) than it is to change our choice of chocolate biscuits.[1]

Persuasive communication designed to change people's attitudes towards other social groups is more like political communication than consumer advertising. People's beliefs about other groups may be deeply rooted, going back to what was learnt as a child. Some research on prejudice suggests that what people believe about other groups may serve a wide range of psychological uses. Many people have a considerable psychological investment in what they believe about others, so that there are very considerable difficulties in changing beliefs by means of the mass media.

But how do people cope when they hear or see something which conflicts with their own deeply held beliefs? The obvious thing to do, is to pay no attention, to turn off the television set or turn over the page. There is plenty of evidence that people do behave in this way, but it is virtually impossible to do this all the time. Willy nilly, we are exposed to all sorts of disagreeable ideas. How do we manage to accommodate notions that go against our beliefs? A number of socio-psychological studies have investigated the effect of mass media materials on people's prejudices.

Eunice Cooper and Helen Dinerman studied how people reacted to an American anti-nazi propaganda film called *Don't be a Sucker*.[2] This film tried to draw parallels between the persecution of minority groups in Nazi Germany and what might happen in the United States. Although most people correctly perceived and accepted the major point of the film, it failed to achieve maximum impact because of the way some of the central ideas were embodied in the fictional characters. For example, the young American, Mike, was first attracted by the words of a street agitator, seen attacking various minority groups, and was then led to see the error of these ideas by a refugee professor. Not unnaturally, several audience members commented that Mike seemed to be very easily led. Mike was supposed to represent openness to reason and eventual tolerance, but he did not come across as a particularly praiseworthy character. On the other hand, Hans, the young German who followed Nazi propaganda, appeared a more sympathetic character (partly because he was played by a well-known actor). Scenes of Hans going off to fight for the Nazis produced the opposite reaction to that intended: 'Hans was regarded not as evil, but as weak, and in fact, as a rather pitiable victim of circumstances.' Even so, *Don't be a Sucker* seems to have got its central anti-prejudice message across to the majority of those who saw it. This does not seem to have happened in two other anti-prejudice campaign studies.

A before-and-after study of anti-Semitic attitudes conducted

E

in connection with showings of the Hollywood feature film *Gentleman's Agreement* suggests that those who were already prejudiced before seeing the film may have become more prejudiced through being exposed to it.[3] Most members of the experimental sample became more favourably disposed towards the Jews, but a small number seem to have used the film to reinforce their own prejudices. Nearly half said they thought the film was propaganda. This group did not become less prejudiced after seeing the film, although there *was* a marked decrease in intolerant responses amongst those who denied that the film was propaganda. The few viewers who said that they were opposed to the production of similar pictures gave much *more* prejudiced answers afterwards. Those who became less prejudiced favoured the making of more films along similar lines. In brief, those who were previously prejudiced against Jews and saw *Gentleman's Agreement* appear to have managed to interpret and use the film to re-inforce their own prejudices. This is a classic example of the 'boomerang' effect. The communication produces opposite results to those intended.

Irwin Rosen has little to say about the mechanisms the prejudiced used to distort the film's message along lines favourable to their own beliefs. This topic is taken up in Eunice Cooper and Marie Jahoda's report of another famous anti-prejudice campaign.[4] These authors describe the reactions of prejudiced individuals to some of the 'Mr. Biggott cartoons', and argue that there was often a 'derailment of understanding'. The cartoon's character showed a ridiculous person with ridiculous anti-minority prejudices. Prejudiced persons seeing the cartoons were supposed to notice similarities between their own prejudices and those of Mr. Biggott, to identify with him, and then to go on to realize the stupidity of both Mr. Biggott's views and their own. However, extended interviews with prejudiced individuals suggested that this process rarely took place. 'Selective perception' became misperception, in terms of the cartoonist's intentions.

Other prejudiced respondents understood the cartoons, but

managed to evade their message in other ways. For example, a series of cartoons ended with the message 'Live and let live'; but many prejudiced people made comments such as 'But it's the Jews that don't let you live; they put themselves outside the rule.' Some prejudiced respondents also discounted dramatized presentations about prejudice on the grounds that they only showed a very special set of circumstances.

These studies tend to show that when unwelcome information is not ignored, it may be turned round and used to confirm and strengthen what the person believed in the first place. In other words, persuasive communication designed to change people's attitudes towards other groups of people, is not merely difficult to achieve (more difficult than effecting a change in brand preference). Such attempts may have just the opposite results to those intended.

The Nature of Prejudice was not designed primarily to change people's attitudes to other social groups. The producers to some degree recognized the difficulties, but they did hope that some new information would be acquired from the programmes. However, while the *producers* had not designed the series to change people's attitudes some reactions to the series showed that this was how some of the *audience* classified the programmes. Some viewers not only misinterpreted the content of the programmes, but their aim as well. This question was not put directly to viewers, so the argument is a deduction from answers given to a range of more detailed questions.

Some of these apparently 'boomerang' effects can be illustrated by reactions to studies of white children shown in Programme II. A relatively neutral comment was 'we can't tell from this work whether coloured children are equally prejudiced or not'. A more critical viewer stated, 'he should have reversed the experiment and found reactions of coloured children to white. This experiment was too one sided.' Another respondent reported the main findings of the experiments as 'white children have a natural affinity to a child of similar appearance. This is rather like a child being at home in its own social group.' This comment avoids any reference to prejudice at all, but supports the behaviour in terms of its naturalness. Half-a-dozen other viewers talked about Dr. Pushkin's experiments in terms of the *positive selection* of white play mates rather than the *negative rejection* of black ones. There is no direct evidence to categorize those who made such comments as prejudiced, but their apparent avoidance of the main point of the research at least suggests how prejudiced viewers might selectively perceive the programme to fit it to their own views.

The making and remaking of Programme VI was described in Chapter 5. This programme showed interviews between the presenter and three 'prejudiced' people. It seemed natural to ask viewers whether they saw these three people as prejudiced or not. Members of the panel were asked to write down statements made by the three speakers with which they agreed. Thirty-three (19%) of the 171 viewers agreed with a prejudiced remark made by James Mottram; 18 (11%) agreed with a prejudiced remark by Lady Dartmouth; but only four (2%) agreed with a prejudiced remark made by Peregrine Worsthorne. These figures suggest that the panel contained a number of viewers who might fairly be labelled as prejudiced in terms of the criteria implicitly defined by the programme itself, and also that the guest whom the production team regarded as *most* prejudiced, was agreed with more often than the other two guests. The way the three prejudiced guests were presented certainly did not prevent some viewers agreeing with them.

Some of the reactions to Programme VI, quoted earlier in this chapter, indicate that some of the viewing panel can be classified as themselves prejudiced, and that such people saw the programme as a threat to their own beliefs.

The commonest defensive action among such viewers seems to have been to launch an attack on the presenter who conducted the interviews. In some cases the threat posed by the programme resulted in anger. One respondent wrote, 'nothing made me angry except perhaps the ineffectiveness of the programme . . . I have developed a prejudice against the presenter and I shall think twice about watching anything in which he appears.' The presenter can perhaps be said to have provided an opening for the various attacks made on him by his pressing and sometimes hostile manner, particularly when interviewing James Mottram. But those who could be classified as prejudiced were significantly more likely to be critical of the presenter than were the non-prejudiced. Of the 22 prejudiced viewers of Programme VI, 13 (59%) were critical of how the presenter handled the interview with James Mottram compared with only 32 (21%) of the non-prejudiced viewers.

Several prejudiced viewers also accused the presenter himself of being prejudiced. The respondent who felt he could 'agree wholeheartedly with the majority of James Mottram's remarks' said in response to another question that the presenter's questioning of James Mottram reflected his basic racial prejudices. Another remarked that 'the presenter was prejudiced in favour of coloured people without accepting many true facts'. This theme, that the series itself was 'guilty' of prejudice in *favour* of certain groups, also emerged in the statement 'the programme itself is prejudiced in favour of the coloured races, and it is trying to influence the people who are filling in this questionnaire in favour of weirdies and coloured peoples'.

One or two prejudiced viewers blamed prejudice on the groups supposedly discriminated against. One respondent wrote, 'the programme has shown that the people that are the most prejudiced are the immigrants themselves. Many of them realize that they are inferior and that integration is almost impossible and hate *us* for being what we are.'

A third defensive tactic was to redefine prejudice so that it appeared to be tolerable, even desirable. One prejudiced viewer wrote, 'the more I see of the programmes the more I ask myself rather impatiently "What is prejudice?" Isn't it a right we have as individuals to feel instinctively for or against things?' Another respondent, who found no evidence in Programme VI that any of the three persons interviewed was prejudiced, also found an escape route by redefining prejudice in a positive way, 'I also refuse to use the pejorative term prejudice for views which are honestly held and for which there is evidence'. Another prejudiced viewer appealed to 'human nature' – 'Prejudices are . . . natural and human . . .' One of the prejudiced adolescent respondents appealed to the 'democratic' right to have personal beliefs, complaining that 'the presenter seems to hint that prejudice is having any views at all'.

Some prejudiced respondents rather than adopting defensive or compensatory tactics managed to perceive the programme selectively and to find positive support for their own beliefs. One viewer gave as the statement from the programme with which he could agree without being prejudiced, 'the majority of immigrants are culturally and educationally inferior to us.' A more moderately toned expression of the same feeling was 'certain prejudices that I had, but had tried to conceal, thinking them to be basically un-Christian, I find myself admitting now more readily. For example, admitting that coloured people are intellectually inferior.' A number of respondents, some of whom could *not* be classified as prejudiced, accepted at face value James Mottram's claim that there is scientific evidence that Negroes are intellectually less far advanced than Caucasians. These differences between the way prejudiced and non-prejudiced viewers reacted to Programme VI proved one of the clearest examples of *differential* responses to *The Nature of Prejudice*. Very many studies of the effects of programmes (or entire mass media campaigns) have shown this kind of inter-action between the programme and the predispositions of different kinds of audience member.

The reactions to *The Nature of Prejudice* reported in this chapter have deliberately been picked to draw attention to where the programmes fell short and to variations in what was communicated. Viewers gave many indications that the programmes interested them. The loyalty of many panel members over a seven-week period itself indicated a considerable degree of involvement.

Nevertheless, it is important to remember from a producer's

or director's point of view, that even a television programme aimed at an audience small by the standards of the medium will still attract a wide variety of people. A programme which is 'just right' for one part of the audience (in terms of prior knowledge, for instance) may be boring or too simple for others. This means that it is difficult to say, in general terms, 'how successful' any programme has been, simply because 'success' is likely to vary widely with different parts of the audience. Producers and directors probably do not think in precise terms about the success of their programmes, but studies of audience reaction provide one of the main kinds of evidence which might lead communicators to define their aims more precisely.

REFERENCES

1. J. Trenaman and D. McQuail, *Television and the Political Image* (London: Methuen) 1961; J. G. Blumler and D. McQuail, *Television in Politics: Its Uses and Influence* (London: Faber & Faber) 1968.

2. E. Cooper and H. Dinerman, 'Analysis of the film *Don't be a Sucker:* a study in communication', *Public Opinion Quarterly*, 15, 1951, pp. 243–264.

3. I. C. Rosen, 'The effect of the motion picture *Gentleman's Agreement* on attitudes towards the Jews', *Journal of Psychology*, 26, 1948, pp. 525–536.

4. E. Cooper and M. Jahoda, 'The evasion of propaganda: how prejudiced people respond to anti-prejudiced propaganda', *Journal of Psychology*, 23, 1947, pp. 15–25.

7

The organization of television production

Previous chapters have followed *The Nature of Prejudice* through the production process from idea to artefact and examined some audience reactions to the series. A change of focus is now necessary in order to investigate the organizational setting and social context within which programme production took place, and to draw out the implications suggested by the case study, for a more general model of mass communication. It hardly needs saying that generalization from this single case is hazardous. Some of its peculiarities can be recognized, for example production took place within one of the commercial companies at a particular point in time. There are clear differences of structure and organization between the commercial companies and the BBC, as well as between individual commercial companies. Other possible peculiarities, for example those resulting from the particular styles used by the individuals involved, are less easy to assess without the further comparative research to which this book looks forward.

THE ORGANIZATION OF WORK

Burns and Stalker in their work on adaptation to change within different industrial companies, draw a distinction between 'mechanistic' and 'organic' systems of management. This contrast is useful to an understanding of the different systems of work organization to be found within a single television organization. In some ways it parallels the distinction between 'creative' and 'technical' personnel which is commonly made within the medium even though several types of work seem to overlap both sides. Burns and Stalker define the two concepts as follows:

In mechanistic systems the problems and tasks facing the concern as a whole are broken down into specialisms. Each individual pursues his task as something distinct from the real tasks of the concern as a whole, as if it were the subject of a sub-contract. 'Somebody at the top' is responsible for seeing to its relevance. The technical methods, duties, and powers attached to each functional role are precisely defined. Interaction within management tends to be vertical, i.e. between superior and subordinate. Operations and working behaviour are governed by instructions and decisions issued by superiors. . .
Organic systems are adapted to unstable conditions, when problems and requirements for action arise which cannot be broken down and distributed among specialist roles within a clearly defined hierarchy. Individuals have to perform their special tasks in the light of their knowledge of the tasks of the firm as a whole. Jobs lose much of their formal definition in terms of methods, duties, and powers, which have to be redefined continually by interaction with others participating in a task. Interaction runs laterally as much as vertically. Communication between people of different ranks tends to resemble lateral consultation rather than vertical command. Omniscience can no longer be imputed to the head of the concern.*

These concepts can be applied to the different styles of work organization exemplified by different groups involved in *The Nature of Prejudice*. Various features of the core production team suggested an organic style of organization. The studio crews who worked on the recording of the programmes fitted into a more mechanistic style, while the camera crew, who carried out the filming, straddled both types. As in Burns and Stalker's own work these contrasting styles of organization

* Burns, T. and Stalker, G. M. *The Management of Innovation*, London, Tavistock 1961, pp. 5–6.

seemed differently suited to deal with change and to handle routine and creative tasks. The work of the camera crew was much less routinized than that of the studio crew. On occasion some of their number were expected to make discretionary decisions. Whereas the production team produced a programme, the studio crew manned a production system, in the same way as other industrial workers on the factory floor.

The Production Team

In summary, the features of the *production team* suggesting an *organic* style of organization were:

1   The team was brought together to work on a particular project for a period of several months. During this time they were largely free from direct control by any other members of the organization. It was accepted that their non-routine, 'creative' task should be carried out independently.

2   Within the team there were different formal roles and an accepted division of function and responsibility. However, there was considerable overlap in the tasks which the members of the group actually performed. The role relationships within the group were loosely defined and changed slightly according to the particular tasks they were engaged on at each stage of the process. Their work was organized around the central goal of getting the programme on the screen, not simply on the performance of any particular task routines.

3   This meant that all the production team identified to some extent with the programme as their work and were interested in it at a substantive level. This is not to contradict the point already made, that the producer was centrally responsible for programme content.

4   Organization within the production team depended very much on personal skills and relationships. General status considerations within the occupational milieu and also

respect for formal role definitions underlay the surface stress on personal relationships. However, during the production the formal basis was rarely used to regulate relationships within the production team. Instead organization depended mainly on the coincidence of personal goals and on their influence on the way members of the team exercised their responsibilities.

5 In most cases financial rewards were a matter of individual negotiation. Status and career rewards could be expected from outside the organization itself reducing the scope for hierarchic control. (This is an extension of the original concept.)

The Studio Crew

The organization of the *studio crew* provided the sharpest contrast and can be labelled *mechanistic*.

1 The crew were regular workers within the production organization, assigned to the continuous performance of the same tasks. The nature and extent of these tasks was formally specified by agreements between management and union and so too were conditions of employment, hours of work, break times and overtime rates.

2 The studio crew's work centred on their particular skills or task routines rather than on the programme. Working on the rota system inhibited any feelings of identification developing with the particular programme or series, though some crew members did mention they had worked on particularly successful and well-known programmes.

3 Although several leading figures in the crew, especially the floor manager, used personal skills to handle relationships within the group, there was rigid adherence to the formal divisions of function and task.

Different *studio crews* worked on each of *The Nature of Prejudice* programmes. They worked a rota in each studio handling whatever programme happened to be booked for recording that day. Physically, the studio was divided into the floor on which production took place and the gallery from which production, sound and lighting were controlled. On the floor each member of the crew had a particular set of tasks to perform. Lacking any detailed knowledge of the programme, they had to be given detailed and routinized instructions on when and how to perform their tasks. Each studio cameraman for example followed a set of shot cards listing the pictures he should take. These were fixed by the director, subject to modification in rehearsal and to flexibility during the studio discussion sessions. Members of the crew remained largely uninvolved with the content of the particular programme. Only once was there widespread interest and reaction from one of the crews working on *The Nature of Prejudice*. That was when Peregrine Worsthorne remarked, in Programme VI, that he did not see how anyone from his background in society could avoid feeling superior to a working man.

Communication between gallery and floor had to be limited mainly to instructions from the former, especially during actual recording. In itself this was one reason for the routinization of task. The floor manager was the important link between the director and the studio crew and performers. He occupied an interstitial role position, representing the director on the studio floor and passing on his instructions, while working regularly with the particular studio crew, as its leader. In this series there was no conflict between the production team and the studio crew, but the former knew the reputations of different floor managers, expecting some to be easier to work with than others. Most of the disagreements which did arise were between the presenter on the studio floor and the rest of the production team, in the gallery. The presenter could not wear headphones and so could only hear the director's instructions as relayed by the floor manager. The floor manager tried to play any disagreements down, relaying only the substance of instructions or questions in either direction. Even so, either side could behave as if they did not really understand the other. The way out was for the director or the presenter to short circuit the relay channel by going down to the floor or up to the gallery after the run through.

The Camera Crew

The *camera crew* who carried out the filming for *The Nature of Prejudice* were also only peripherally involved with the programmes. Only the production team discussed the film sequences after they had been shot in terms of their implications for the programmes and their content. In the rest periods between filming, the technical personnel made very little reference to the film or the subject matter of the programmes in general. References to prejudice did occur on the first morning of filming and on the third morning, when the crew first moved to the ATV studio. These were all joking references and apparently served to link the group around the common task. Members of the camera crew, for this production mainly the cameraman, were called on to take more discretionary decisions in the course of their work than members of the studio crew. It appeared that such decisions had to be based more on technical skill and specialized occupational criteria than on the substance of the programme.

The cameraman was the main link between the production team and the camera crew in both work and non-work situations. For example, only the cameraman sat with the production team when the two groups separated for lunch. Most members of the crew were simply supplied by a free-lance agency, but the producer and director specified the cameraman by name. They expected the one they picked to be technically competent, without insisting on an idiosyncratic visual style or interfering with production decisions. While filming, the formal chain of command ran from the producer, through the director, through the cameraman to the crew, though, as might be expected, this was not strictly followed.

Virtually all film follows the same path from shooting to

cutting and editing, so a camera crew is likely to be as well informed as other production personnel on the film techniques necessary to meet later requirements. This is a potential source of conflict between the camera crew and a producer or director. If the latter appear ignorant of how to film to make later cutting and editing possible, members of the camera crew may feel particularly resentful, because of the contrast between themselves and production personnel in rewards, social status, technical training and recruitment. There was a feeling among the camera crew that some people attracted to television were simply university graduates with little idea what else to do. Such tension did not appear in the production of *The Nature of Prejudice*, but was reported by the camera crew as part of their working experience.

Another source of tension is that production teams are often intensely involved in their programmes, working round the clock for short periods to get the film they want. Once filming is over the production team has a chance to relax, but the camera crew moves to a new production with a different production team, who may expect just as much effort as the first. Union restrictions on hours of work and high overtime rates may not only enable crew members to earn more money, but also serve to protect them from a producer or director who thinks his is the only series in production.

As stated, the important features of working within television for members of the *production team* was the lack of organizational routine. The producer was the leader of the team, setting the others' work load. His production style was unfamiliar to some of the team, who were used to a more routinized process similar to that outlined in the adult education phase (Chapter 2). This difference caused anxiety within the team as, very often the director and the researcher did not know what the producer had planned for later programmes in the series. There were discussions within the team on the series and its subject, but these were more occasions for airing personal opinions than planning sessions. The producer took little part in them.

One pertinent illustration of how tension can arise when roles are loosely defined centred on the work of the p.a. The producer allowed the p.a. to take considerable part in programme discussions. The director expected the p.a. to be a docile and attractive assistant, working for the director more than the producer. In this case however the p.a. worked more for the producer than the director. Apparently this reflected her judgement of their relative importance and influence. In discussions she was always ready to give her opinion, even on topics which were strictly the director's responsibility. Before the studio production stage the director himself had worked mainly as assistant to the producer, without any special role of his own. This conflict did reach the point when the director invoked the formal job definitions laid down by the trade union, in the process stopping a film editing session. Therefore, in the last resort formal definitions could be invoked.

Some of the styles of behaviour adopted by the production personnel showed the importance of personal, particularistic relationships in the occupational milieu. Theatrical language, with its epithets of personal endearment, was used by all of the production team some of the time and by some of the production team all of the time. This personal affective language seemed to be important in enabling the team to work together and to include the other individuals who were only peripherally involved for short periods. As production was mainly carried out in small groups the language provided a pseudo-*gemeinschaft* within which relationships could be managed, and any conflicts and tensions eased.

The occupational milieu also cut across the organizational hierarchy, providing other status qualifications apart from role and position within the organization and offering other career goals. Developing a personal reputation within the occupational milieu or a public *persona* in the wider society not only fostered an individual's own employment opportunities but also made him an attractive colleague with whom others would wish to work. Members of *The Nature of Prejudice* production team all had different personal goals. The producer's career in programme production was a relatively new departure following his career in broadcasting administration. He also had literary interests outside his television work. The presenter was emerging from a period in which he had been in eclipse to regain a place as a leading television personality. The director was most closely committed to ATV as a company, looking forward to continuing work on similar programmes within the same department. In contrast both the p.a. and the researcher were hoping to move to other types of work in other organizations.

Four of these five were employed on free-lance contracts. The development of free-lancing is itself an important structural reason for the emphasis placed on personal contacts and relationships within the occupational milieu of television. In the case of *The Nature of Prejudice*, for example, personal knowledge about their availability and competence played a part in the selection of all members of the production team. The personal mechanisms were least important in the case of the p.a. who was allocated by the administrative system within the company; most obvious in the case of the researcher, who was recommended to the producer by the executive producer, for whom she had previously been working. Although there was a distinction within the company between contract and staff researchers, little attempt was made to allocate them to programmes according to their specialized abilities, past experience or through other more bureaucratic processes. Instead the system depended mainly on personal allocation and patronage.

Another illustration of the importance of these mechanisms were the many informal discussions within *The Nature of Prejudice* team on who was working where and what series were currently in production in other companies. Similarly the film crew, who were also employed free-lance, spent much of the time between filming discussing possible employment opportunities and the current whereabouts of colleagues. Networks of informal personal contact across the industry appear to be built up by the very job mobility which they facilitate.

THE CONTEXT OF PROGRAMME PRODUCTION

The growth of free-lancing in British television since 1954 also seems to have had other general consequences for the relationship between production personnel, employing organizations and their executives. The system offers successful individuals the possibilities of higher earnings and allows them freedom to move from company to company to work out their ideas. The companies benefit too by economizing on 'creative personnel', who can be hired as necessary for a particular job. More significant, however, are such possible general effects as increased insecurity and competition, increased opportunities for hiring new talent and retiring old. When *The Nature of Prejudice* was in production there did seem to be a tendency for individual free-lancers to become closely associated with one or two companies, developing and maintaining contacts with relevant departmental heads. However, free-lancing could widen a divide between company executives hiring labour, and mobile production personnel, unable to establish a continuing, collaborative base within any organization from which to develop distinctive styles of creative work. Fear of such a development has grown recently as the economic situation within the medium has worsened.

But, if free-lancing limits the power of the creative personnel, it also has the opposite effect of limiting the range of sanctions and influences which an executive producer can bring to bear on a producer, or a producer on other members of a production team. In the long run other opportunities may be available for employment once the present production is finished, and similar employment opportunities may not be in the gift of those controlling the current production. In the short run those in control want to see the production process completed. They have to judge how far they can intervene without causing others to walk out on the production. In the case of *The Nature of Prejudice* fear of such an eventuality appeared to be real, in the sense that it was mentioned as a guiding principle of production relationships. There was no indication, however, that a walk out was ever likely. One reason why the producer readily deferred to the presenter's judgement on the studio floor was because he feared that the presenter might abandon the programmes at the last moment. (Again there was no direct indication that the presenter was prepared to do so.) On the other hand, one reason why the presenter was prepared to intervene positively was because his reputation was the first at risk if the programmes were not successful on the screen.

Different executive producers vary widely in the way they interpret their role and in the relationship they establish with the producer, leading the team. In some cases the executive producer may be closely involved, planning the programme and only leaving the producer the job of collecting the material. In this case, however, the executive producer set the conditions within which the producer had to work, principally the budget and the screening deadline, and left the producer to work out his own ideas with the production team. He kept himself generally informed about the progress of the series, but he did not directly intervene until it was obvious something had gone wrong with Programme VI. In the course of these discussions he also took a closer interest in planning for Programme VII. But in both cases he accepted the producer's aims for the programme, trying to suggest ways in which they might be more successfully realized. The screening deadline provided the best example of an implicit supervisory technique used by the executive producer. The limited time available not only helped to structure possible production alternatives, it also helped to keep the production moving.

Even though the production team appeared to be independent of outside surveillance and control, there were several indications that they worked within an accepted framework of assumptions. This is hardly surprising. The producer was allowed independence because it could be assumed both that he knew how to do the job and the 'rules of the game' within which it had to be accomplished.

One aspect of this framework was the need to avoid libel and other legal problems. For example the producer's desire for a dramatic confrontation in Programme VI (one between Sir Cyril Osborne and a Black Power spokesman was contemplated) was tempered by his fear of allowing libellous statements (as well as other considerations such as whether it would work on television). The producer accepted that any 'outrageous' content or especially controversial statements should be referred to the executive producer to ensure his backing.

This led to caution in contacting extreme examples of prejudice; but caution of a different type was shown in presenting the prejudiced views finally included. The producer adopted a neutral production role which meant he refrained from saying directly in the programmes which items he believed to be examples of prejudice. Most of the statements by James Mottram, the interviewee most frequently used to illustrate prejudiced opinion, were obliquely disassociated from the programme to show that they were intended as examples of prejudice. Such disassociation ranged from a single phrase, for example 'so called'; through extended statements of a different view, for example, in Programme III, 'even if black and white and brown rats are as hostile to each other as is claimed, what about black and white and brown rabbits?'; to a film clip of football fans being 'unrestrained' countering Mottram's claim that whereas negroes are 'uninhibited', British people are 'sober in their tastes and very restrained'. In this last case the producer felt he had deserted his normal role to make a definite point visually. In most cases, however, the items were labelled as prejudices for those who could follow the oblique, implicit disassociations. These created conditions for a form of 'in-group' communication.

In a sense, some of the production team's basic assumptions about prejudice and how to tackle it suggested that they felt themselves to belong to a wider 'in-group' extending beyond the occupational milieu of television to include other members of the educated middle class. James Mottram was unique in so far as he was a member of that class who did not share the fundamental, liberal-rational value position. This underlay the production team's basic view that prejudice was reprehensible, a view supported both by colleagues in the medium and by most of the academics contacted for the programme. Some of the informal discussions within the production team about prejudice could be interpreted as attempts to establish this basic value position, and to work out how it would apply to particular cases. The production philosophy adopted for the series of 'evidence' leading to 'conclusions', reflected the same fundamental set of liberal values, as well as the 'in-group' communication problem. Those who shared the values could be expected to draw the right conclusions. Those outside the liberal middle class consensus probably would not, but the position itself seemed to lead inevitably to the view that that was their problem, a problem with which the programmes could not be expected to deal directly.

However, liberal-rational assumptions were coloured by more specific assumptions related to the medium of television itself. A basic premise of the whole series, laid down in the adult education phase, was that it should not concentrate exclusively on race and colour but should deal with the phenomenon in the round. This was constantly reiterated by production personnel at all levels throughout the process. Among the reasons which may be suggested for this was a feeling that colour prejudice had been well-aired already. A series on it would be nothing new and the viewers might well become bored. Race and colour were also recognized as the most controversial aspect of the subject, involving considerable risk of antagonizing the audience. Except for the prestige to be gained from documentary production, the company had little to gain, and potentially much to lose, if audience reaction was hostile to a series dealing with such a sensitive subject.

One of the peculiar historical circumstances surrounding the production of *The Nature of Prejudice* was that in the period before the reallocation of commercial television contracts in

1968, current affairs and documentary production became un-usually important as a source of prestige with the ITA. One of the two associate heads of ATV's Factual Programme Depart-ment, the executive producer on *The Nature of Prejudice*, had been appointed explicitly to earn the company a reputation for documentary production. Formally, the department received an annual budget, based largely on an updating of the budget for the previous year, but during this period the executives could expect direct support for their plans and proposals from the top management. The appointment of two associate heads of parallel power and status in this department was an indi-cation of other conflicts and goals within the company. Two factions were competing for control of the company at board level. The executives and department heads were generally known to be lined up with one side or the other. The two heads of the Factual Programme Department were each associated with different factions. This peculiar set of circumstances played some part in helping the executive producer to put through the plans for the series.

But in many ways isolation and autonomy were the most striking characteristics of the production team's situation, re-flected not only in the lack of organizational control but also in the haphazard, particularistic processes of programme pro-duction, discussed in earlier chapters. The executive producer had the general responsibility of linking the production team to wider environments within which they worked. The press releases and the *TV Times* billings were all checked by the executive producer as well as the producer, the director and the company press officer. Similarly when the ITA intervened to check on Programme I, it was the executive producer as much as the producer who prepared to defend it. Officers at the ITA had been worried by a press report about the first programme from which it appeared that it might be racially defamatory. Arrangements were made for them to see the programme and although the executive producer and the other executive in the department were ready to defend it there was no need as the

ITA officers were satisfied with what they saw. This threat of interference from outside the company, let alone outside the production team, led to strong feelings of internal cohesion in the department.

Another aspect of the autonomy of the production team was their separation from the audience. There was a considerable gap between studio recording and transmission. The production team had disbanded before all the series had been seen by the viewers. First, among the four main types of audience reaction available to the production team were a few brief newspaper criticisms. The critics did not provide any detailed analysis of these programmes or any ideas on how they might have been differently produced.

Second, each programme produced some unsolicited correspondence, averaging about ten letters per programme.* Many of these letters came from people who appeared to have used *The Nature of Prejudice* production team simply as a convenient third person on whom they could work out their personal problems. After an opening sentence or two these letters usually had no further links at all with the programmes, a fact which made the task of classifying the letters particularly difficult, although they were included in Table 1.

As can be seen from Table 1, a minority of all letters came from people who liked the programmes or were neutral about them. Most of the eleven letters which were favourable to the programmes were straightforward 'fan' letters for the presenter. The largest group of 'neutral' letters came from people working on educational projects who wrote to enquire whether the producer could supply them with material or contacts. Looking at the letters in terms of the author's apparent purpose only nine correspondents made concrete suggestions about the production of the programmes. These were mostly hostile to the

* The production team broke up before all the series was transmitted and though letters to later programmes were collected, there is reason to believe some were missed. There is no reason to suppose that those collected were not representative.

TABLE 1

AUDIENCE LETTERS

Subject matter of letter	No.	General attitude
Shows prejudice against black people	27	Hostile
Shows prejudice against young people	3	
Reacts that programme itself prejudiced	4	
Likes/approves of programme and/or presenter	11	Favourable
Requests for information	7	Neutral
Offers of help	2	
Discusses issues raised by programme	6	
Other – mainly vehicles for personal problems	5	
Total	65	

Writer's Inferred Purpose

To make concrete programme suggestions, e.g. other people to interview	9
To give ideas about prejudice, quasi-research ideas	3
To emphasize own position pro-programme	5
To emphasize own position anti-programme	34
Cranks and others	14
Total	65

series from people who felt their viewpoint, particularly on the colour question, had been ignored. Nearly half of all letters were written by people hostile to coloured immigrants, who opposed what they saw as the general liberalism of the programmes. The production team had expected that the series would provoke a great deal of hostile correspondence from people, using the terms discussed above, outside the 'in-group' of the liberal, educated, middle class. The unsolicited correspondence brought in by *The Nature of Prejudice* confirmed this expectation. It was no use to the production team in suggesting programme ideas for the future, because of its content, the way the team reacted to it and because by the time most of it arrived, the production team had disbanded and each member was working with another team on a new programme.

The third contact which the production team had with their audience was through the audience viewing figures. At that time these came from TAM. The director was used to working on similar Sunday afternoon programmes and had a general idea of what audience figure to expect. He hoped for an audience figure above average that would show they had made 'as big a stir as possible' by achieving publicity for the series. This attitude was not strongly endorsed by the producer.

Finally, the production team were themselves able to watch the programmes as viewers. This was the main source of comments when the first programmes were discussed within the team after they had been transmitted. In addition the team collected comments from others – colleagues within the medium or friends outside. It is hardly surprising that such comments were collected and reported selectively. They were either used to substantiate an individual's own opinion or else they were cited as examples of how wrong people who were not 'in the know' could be. This is not to say that members of the production team would not make or accept criticisms. Some were strongly critical of parts of the programmes they had made. The point is simply that because of the way the production team was separated from all but a select and distorted sample of audience reactions, such criticisms had to be based in the first instance on the individual's own reaction to re-viewing the programme. Any information the individual possessed about audience reaction could then be fed in to substantiate the opinion, or if it appeared to conflict a reason could usually be found for ignoring or invalidating it.*

* This seems to be one function – though by no means the only one – of such widely held production beliefs as 'TV critics know nothing about the real work and problems of production' or 'most viewers who write letters are psychopaths'. So far as the viewers are concerned another function appears to be to emphasize that they do not belong to the same socio-cultural group as the production personnel.

This account of the organization of television at programme production level has stressed the apparent autonomy of the production team both within the organization and in relation to their audience and the rest of society. The organization set a framework within which the production team worked and provided them with resources and facilities. In earlier chapters we suggested that programme content tended to be a latent consequence of decisions taken for other reasons. This chapter has shown that, because of the organic style of work organization found in the production team, the course of the production process depended on the coincidence of personal goals and the development of personal relationships. The producer and the others in the production team were left to interpret their brief within the organization, with few directives on the shape and content of the final programmes. As important, perhaps more important for the production personnel than the context set by the organization was the occupational milieu of television and the broader liberal, educated middle class background which embraced it. The production team were far from being, as some have depicted them, alienated processors of routine material for programmes in an established genre. Different styles of work organization within the television company also suggested some of the ways in which such organizations might differ from a bureaucratic, rationalized model. Two types of work process are involved, programme production and the production of material artefacts. Nevertheless, we have seen in earlier chapters how programme production was guided by a number of occupational routines and accepted practices. We must now examine some of the possibilities of communication through the medium of television which these routines allow and analyse the roles of producer and audience in the general mass communication process.

8

Mass communication – a contradiction in terms?

One aim in case study research is to move from the particular to the general. This chapter presents an account of the production process for television abstracted from the case study reported above and drawing on other studies to show how they contribute to the overall argument. It looks forward to further research on other types of programmes to fill out the general picture. The more speculative parts of the analysis presented in this chapter are included in the hope they will stimulate such research. Meanwhile that already completed suggests some extremely important propositions about the nature and scope of communication possible through a mass medium like television. These raise specific questions about the type of content which can be expected from a medium of mass communication, as well as wider questions about the modes of communication possible within societies dominated by such mass media and the possible consequences of these for social structure and process.

This chapter will extend the view introduced at the start of this book: the mass media and the professional communicators who work within them as crucial intermediaries between the society as source and the society as audience. This intermediary role cannot be seen simply as a passive channel of information flow, as implied by the 'gatekeeper' model and its derivatives. Nor are the intermediaries purposive communicators in the terms suggested by the persuasive models of the communication process. But the actions of such communicators do result in the creation of an image of social reality which includes both cognitive and evaluative elements. The cognitive elements are drawn from a limited range of sources in society, processed through occupational and technological routines and presented to add to a separate and self-supporting media culture. It acquires an evaluative dimension through the elaboration of symbols and definitions within it, identifying particular social groups and their positions on particular social issues.

The concept of media culture suggests support for McCormack's argument that in modern society the output of the mass media can be seen as drawing on and reinforcing a collective, integrative *gestalt*.[1] But there are important limitations on the communicator's ability to elaborate and communicate substantive meaning through television. On the account of television production developed through the case study material, it seems likely that the output of the medium will lack the planning and the integration implied by McCormack's phrase. An essential feature of media culture is its ability to embrace confused and contradictory positions. Television does not provide society with an homogeneous integrative *gestalt* so much as with a variety of ways of managing and assimilating knowledge and opinion, in some cases by presenting and reinforcing established perspectives, in others by challenging or cancelling particular points of view.

THE LIMITS ON COMMUNICATION IN TELEVISION DOCUMENTARY PRODUCTION

A variety of factors inhibit communication through television. They may be grouped under four main headings: relationships with sources; the division of labour at different production stages; the relationship with the audience; and organizational or communicator control. The central position of the producer as leader of the production team has emerged from the analysis of the production of the documentary series, *The Nature of*

Prejudice. To an extent he created the final output. One of the three chains which generated and supported ideas for the programmes – the subject chain – was firmly based on the producer's ideas and past experiences. However, the other two chains – the presentation and the contact chain – placed two limitations on the producer's creative role. Material had to be suitable and available for television presentation. These two chains did more than limit what the producer could achieve. They themselves generated ideas and items for programme content. The contact chain shows one way in which the professional communicator is dependent on the society in which he works. The presentation chain emphasizes the requirements of the medium and the development of particular methods and standards of production within it.

The three contact mechanisms included within the contact chain played a particularly important part in limiting the range of material available for television production. The range of material is heavily weighted towards ideas about a subject, previously elaborated through the culture of the mass media. Television, the press and other media played a large part in making a particular set of people, events and previously prepared material available for *The Nature of Prejudice* series. The case of Programme VI, discussed above, provides a particularly clear example of the way in which the production team was forced to use media channels and to draw on their experience of a general media culture to find the people they wanted to appear in the programmes. Through these various mechanisms a new production draws on the established culture of the media, thus ensuring similarity and continuity in the view of the world presented. Nevertheless, they also show the large part which chance plays in the process. Chance occurs within a bounded system.

This picture of the media culture as a largely separate and self-contained system is further supported by the use made of the other two contact mechanisms, personal acquaintance and organizations. The personal acquaintances of production personnel are built up through working in the medium and through contacting sources for other productions. Organizations, especially representative ones such as those used in *The Nature of Prejudice*, are outside the media culture but available for use by it. In many cases these organizations have a view they want to put across. They are likely to want to be purposive communicators in terms of the Westley-Maclean model.[2] But their ability to be purposive or persuasive is limited by the intermediary role of the professional communicator. Occasionally, through constant contact and exposure, their view is incor-porated as an accepted part of the conventional wisdom of the media culture. Such examples are rare, because the purpose of many organizations is to put forward views in sensitive areas. These cannot be accepted as they stand because the communicator and the institution in which he is employed are required to be impartial. At this point the factor of *organizational or communicator control* appears.

A more usual process than the incorporation of the views of a particular group and one which was illustrated in *The Nature of Prejudice*, is the incorporation of publicized expert opinion on issues too global to be directly subject to the rules of political partiality. The 1967 Reith Lectures had the effect of elevating Edmund Leach, the lecturer, to the status of *global thinker*. Suddenly he was in great demand throughout television as a guest-speaker. Similar processes on an even larger scale can be seen in the treatment given to Desmond Morris following the publication of *The Naked Ape*. Clearly these processes of cultural change require much more detailed investigation than is possible here. The main conclusion to be drawn from the present study is that television production tends to ensure cultural repetition and continuity. On many subjects which might be treated by television, and on most which are continually regarded as news, there seem to be standard perspectives available within the media culture which are likely to be reinforced and repeated in the process of gathering material for a new programme.[3] The question we are left with is what are the conditions a new perspective has to meet in order to be taken up by the media?

The problem of partiality is only one of the hurdles such a new perspective would have to clear. A second is the desire of the production personnel to avoid control or influence from outsiders, including sources. This can be demonstrated from the findings of another study of a television documentary, this time on cancer research. In that study, research scientists and doctors specializing in the treatment of cancer with radiotherapy were interviewed for their views on television publicity for cancer research and for their reactions to the particular programme.[4] The scientists and doctors held two rather different views of cancer research. The scientists stressed the need for basic scientific work, the doctors the more immediate returns to be expected from empirical manipulation of treatment techniques. Both these can be seen as professional ideologies, in the terms used by Strauss and others, based on and justifying the different features of their professional work.[5] But both groups, and especially the leading scientists and doctors in their public capacities, also subscribed to an over-arching ideology which stressed that cancer was not, as popularly imagined, a terrifying, unknown killer. They pointed to the way in which education and diagnosis facilities might breach the vicious circle of public fear which kept death rates high. These three ideologies, and especially the third which was used widely for public consumption in other fields, show the way in which television's potential sources could make sense of the field of cancer research.

The television documentary, however, did not adopt any of these views. Instead, it presented a picture of cancer research in which a variety of points of view were reflected, but none presented or developed as a coherent view of the subject. The final section of the programme, for example, consisted of statements from prominent research scientists on the likely rate of progress in research. These varied wildly, but they were simply laid side by side in the programme with no attempt to judge

between them. Another feature of the content of the programme – the number of sequences picturing research with
animals – shows the way the selection criteria of the professional communicators were superimposed on the views of
their sources. The use of animals in research was one aspect of
a complex scientific problem which the audience could be expected to understand and react to. Further the scientists, although they did not attempt to restrict the material available to
the communicators, tried to discourage the portrayal of animals
as they feared repercussions from an emotional public. This
type of material, therefore, both fitted the communicator's idea
of 'good television' and enabled them to assert their independence from their sources.

This study also shows the important difference between
presenting a picture of a subject through television and making
sense of it, by providing a coherent account. Many of the
scientists had experience in giving public talks or lectures on
research. They criticized the programme for not giving simple,
logical accounts of the research problem and the way it was
being tackled. Conversely, they approved of one section of the
programme which did 'tell a story' about a particular cancer
and the attempts which had been made to control it. The use
the professional communicators made of the medium, showing
animals and complex research machinery for their visual appeal
and because they fitted a special musical score, seem to have
inhibited the development of a coherent story approach such
as the scientists advocated. Moreover, the professional communicators were not expert in the field which they proposed to
cover. They could hardly be expected to become conversant
with a complex subject in the space of time it took to make a
television programme. This is another form of the dilemma discussed in the adult education phase of *The Nature of Prejudice*
– the choice between a subject expert, and an expert in the
television medium. The communicators' non-expert status,
their production criteria, the nature of the medium, their desire
to keep their distance from their sources, and their beliefs about

audience reactions, all inhibited a coherent account of the subject emerging through the television programme.

Such factors are reinforced by others following from the basic legal structure within which the communicator operates. Two which have been illustrated in the analysis of *The Nature of Prejudice* are the need to avoid libel and to ensure balance and impartiality. One common technique for handling the requirement of impartiality is to ensure that any view is matched by its opposite. Another technique for handling such problems is to attribute views to outside parties, thus absolving the communicator from responsibility. This technique of attribution to an outside source is one commonly used in news bulletins where there are differences of opinion over the facts of a case.[6] A producer seems more likely to adopt a particular point of view when it has been previously put forward by others in the media and so sanctioned as part of the conventional media culture. The evidence needed to support a known perspective will be much slimmer than that required to support a new and different point of view.

But as well as working through sources, the television producer has to work through a variety of other intermediaries who stand between himself and the society as source. This is the problem identified above as *the division of labour inherent at different stages of television production*. On *The Nature of Prejudice* it was always possible for the producer to deal directly with a source, though, as Diagram 1 demonstrates, contact mechanisms and other intermediaries were usually necessary for the producer to reach a source of useful material. 'Vox Pops' provide perhaps the best example of a direct approach to 'people in society', and they show the inherent inadequacy and fortuitousness of this method of finding material. The production personnel recognizing the editorial control which could be exercised by intermediaries and sources tried to get as close to their material as possible. But the more distanced they were from the source, the more likely they were to use material already accepted within the media culture because they were dependent on other people's understandings of their ideas and purposes.

The producer had to work through others not only to collect ideas and material, but also to realize those ideas on the screen. Each separate specialist involved in this process had his own set of standards for judging and selecting material. These were based on his own particular skills and so might vary from those of the producer. The way in which this could contribute to a reduction in the meaning of the programme content is best

DIAGRAM 1

PRODUCER, INTERMEDIARIES AND SOURCES

	Production team	*Contact mechanisms*	*Other intermediaries*	*Sources*
	Director	Press	Organization leaders	People in society
Producer		Organizations		
	Researcher			Events in society
		Personal		
			Controllers of material e.g. librarians	Previously prepared media material

illustrated in the role played by the programme presenter. On occasion the presenter 'took the role of the audience' in order to suggest cuts, simplifications and adaptations to make the content more appealing to an average audience member. His knowledge about such an average audience member was necessarily tenuous and speculative. But regardless of the characteristics attributed to the imagined audience, the concern in this process seemed to be not with simpler and so more effective communication of meaning, but with simplification in order to ensure that audience attention was not lost. In other words, the aim was to establish a relationship between production and audience based on audience satisfaction rather than the com-

F

munication of meaning. Of course audience attention is an essential precondition to the communication of meaning and the producer of *The Nature of Prejudice* thought that, realistically, he could only hope to put across a few simple points to an audience varying greatly in intelligence and educational experience.

The use of 'live' studio discussions in television programmes illustrates another way in which the actual process of television production tends to reduce the meaning contained in the output. Some of the points already made generally apply specifically to 'live' discussions, for example, the tendency to challenge guest opinion and to use a panel rather than a single guest. A panel both ensures variety of view and insures against a guest who does not come over well on television. But a panel discussion is liable to limit the scope allowed to any guest to develop an account or an argument. In such a discussion the presenter has a difficult role to play, drawing out the views of a guest but at the same time representing the viewer and summarizing or simplifying on his behalf. Discussions also aim to be attractive spectacles in which the participants challenge each other or engage in conversational repartee. The premium on brief, simple expression makes for a reliance on conventional points or illustrations in the argument. In *The Nature of Prejudice* this was again well illustrated in Programme VI. The presenter's reference to 'the way Hitler used to talk about the Jews' or Lady Dartmouth's claim that she would 'fight to the death for the freedom of the individual' are two particularly clear examples of participants using conventional phrases with wide cultural and symbolic overtones. They are further examples of the general perspectives available in the media culture which are associated with evaluative reaction as well as cognitive meaning. The general tendency, whether in explanatory or combative discussions, seems to be towards encounters which follow a simple and predictable form, as if each side was making moves in a game. The more the subject recurs in the media, the more it is embedded in the media culture.

A Typology of Televisual Communication

These various processes through which meaning is controlled in television documentary production all suggest important ways in which the medium and its output are managed and assimilated within the social structure. But, before considering that problem further, it is worth trying to widen the horizons of the discussion from documentary production to include other types of production for television. In documentary production the professional communicator has a part to play as a creative intermediary between source and audience. In the course of the study of *The Nature of Prejudice* this type of production was contrasted with the system used to produce adult education programmes. Material was funnelled into the visual and verbal forms necessary to make a television programme. 'Funnelled' seems the best word to describe a system in which the material was taken from sources outside television and then passed through a series of specialized processes to fit it for presentation on the screen. Although the television personnel still retain authority over their sources in this case it seems qualitatively different from the documentary production system in which the television producer takes his own view of the subject matter, albeit in interaction with the material available to him.

The contrast between these two production systems suggests that one continuum underlying different types of production for television is the varying scope of the producer's role.* This continuum is set out on the left hand side of Diagram 2.† Party political broadcasts and 'one shot' plays are examples of programmes which might be expected to come at opposite extremes of such a continuum. In the first case the role of the television producer is limited to making technical facilities available to communicators outside the medium, in the second the terminology of production and source ceases to be relevant and we

---

* In this context and throughout the rest of this chapter, producer is used as a general term to include all those involved in production within television.
† See p. 155.

are dealing with a case much closer to the high cultural model of artistic creativity. Compared with these two both documentaries and adult education programmes come towards the centre of the continuum. News programmes can also be fitted into this framework. Newsmen do not re-create their view of a subject in the same way as a documentary producer, but they do have important decisions to take on selection and presentation. A recent study of the television news coverage of a particular event – the Anti-Vietnam War Demonstrations of 27th October, 1968, showed that bulletins produced some time after the event were more like television programmes made to retell the story as the newsmen had seen it than those which were put out while the event was still going on.[7] This had important consequences for the way the story was structured and interpreted in later bulletins. In other words even with a single type of production, there is likely to be some variation in its place on the continuum, in this case according to the time and resources allowed for making the programme.

It should be clear, however, that this continuum, based on the scope allowed to television production, has important implications for the relationship of the medium to the society as source. A parallel continuum based on this is shown on the right of the diagram. The more limited the scope of television production the more direct the access of the society as source to the society as audience. Party politicals are a comparatively rare example of direct access being allowed to persuasive communicators outside the medium. Other examples of direct access include sports programmes and outside broadcasts, neither of which usually deals with purposive communicators or persuasive subjects. Programmes, designed to deal regularly with a specific subject for a minority audience or to cater for a particular audience need such as religious programming or adult education broadcasts, offer the purposive communicators in each field – the clerics and the educators – a more modified form of access. In both cases special institutional machinery has been set up to link television production with interested parties

DIAGRAM 2

A TYPOLOGY OF MASS COMMUNICATION

Scope of production	Production function	Example programme type	Access of society as source	Audience relationship
Limited	Technical facilitation	Party political	Direct	Persuasive-effectiveness
	Facilitation, selection	Adult education	Modified Direct	Informative-effectiveness
	Selection, presentation	News bulletin	Filtered	Informative-satisfaction
	Selection, compilation	Documentary	Remade	Satisfaction, informative
	Realization, creation	'Realistic' Serial	Advisory	Satisfaction, entertainment
Extensive	Creation, origination	'One Shot' Plays	Uncontrolled	Artistic satisfaction

in the particular field. But in both cases television producers have retained ultimate control over programme production. In the field of religious broadcasting, for example, there has been a continual search for programmes which would fill the religious 'closed period' on Sunday evening but which at the same time would not be branded with a religious label, and so have a wider appeal than the committed religious audience. This seems a particularly good example of the professional communicator trying to develop the mass characteristics of the medium and the potential of his own role even in an area which had been to some extent insulated for a minority audience.

These examples suggest that there are comparatively few cases of direct or modified-direct access through television to the audience for purposive or persuasive communicators. It is also interesting to note that, with the exception of party political broadcasts, there seems to be an inverse relationship between access for outsiders and the amount of resources, and the size of audience made available in television. Adult education programmes, for example, are generally given a small budget and placed in unattractive time-slots. This point can of course be argued both ways. Programmes allowing direct access are likely to be less attractive to viewers than those made by professional communicators, because they are attempts to use the most mass of media for minority purposes.

Proceeding along the continuum: the greater the scope of the television producer's role, the more limited the access available for the society as source to the society as audience. In news bulletins, information about people and events in society comes filtered through the selection and presentation decisions made by television newsmen. Their ideas on what makes news decide which people and issues will receive publicity through the medium. Purposive communicators often supported by public relations specialists can attempt to manipulate the news media by trading on these criteria or by bringing pressure to bear on the newsroom to change the criteria in their favour. Some politicians, par excellence Senator Joseph McCarthy, have been outstandingly successful at news management. This is a danger of which newsmen themselves are very well aware.[8] They are also aware of attempts by politicians to pressure them into changing the rules of the game. The central point, however, is that access through this type of programme is allowed on the media's terms. At another level it is then possible to explain the terms offered according to the occupational and organizational situation of the journalists and of their place with the news media in the social structure.

Most research on mass communication which has dealt with problems of production and process has concentrated on non-fictional output. The data reported in this study has been no exception. The attempt made to extend the two continua in Diagram 2 into the field of fictional programmes and dramatic productions is even more speculative than the rest of this discussion. The typology outlined in Diagram 2 probably suffers from a phenomenon familiar to social scientists in other fields – that it is easy to make fine discriminations when dealing with subjects on which information is available and to fall back on more general categories when the subject matter is less familiar. The types of dramatic programme shown in Diagram 2 – realistic series and 'one-shot' plays – are included to give an example of the type of discrimination which it might be possible to make in this area. A more comprehensive typology must await further work on these and similar programmes.

The term 'realistic series' is intended to include programmes based on known communities or occupations. Such series are often equipped with an expert adviser whose task is to keep creative imagination within realistic bounds. Moreover, the community or occupation concerned is likely to take an interest in how it is portrayed in the programmes. Its success in influencing the production personnel and the television organizations will depend on a variety of factors such as the strength of any representative organizations and the social standing of the group concerned. In contrast 'one-shot' plays seem to be more simply a matter for the writer and the television production team to originate and create as they think best. It is a moot point whether the author of such plays should be regarded as inside or outside the medium.

MEDIA, AUDIENCE AND SOCIETY

It should be clear that although this typology of different programme types has been presented as if each type was a distinct, homogeneous category, considerable variation is to be expected between different programmes in each type. Drawing on the contrast between communication and satisfaction or communication and attention which has been made on several occasions above, it is possible to introduce another set of terms to explain some of the differences between and within the programme types outlined in Diagram 2. To do so the concepts of communication, attention and satisfaction need further consideration.

The aim of the persuasive communicator, the party political broadcaster or the advertiser, is to change or confirm attitudes and behaviour. The principal criterion against which their communications should be judged is persuasive effectiveness. Although we have suggested that various features of the production process in television militate against it, it is possible that professional communicators working on non-fictional programmes will be concerned with informative effectiveness, that is in using the medium for the effective communication of meaning. In the case study, although there were elements of such an approach behind some production decisions, these appeared to be over-ruled by a contrasting orientation towards audience attention. It is clear that any production team is likely to have a mixed orientation, but the aim of this study has been to isolate the main tendencies inherent in production for the medium.

Discussion of the relationship between fictional programmes and the audience is subject to the same reservations already made above. Nevertheless, Hall and Whannel's contrast between high art, popular art, and mass media art shows sufficient similarity to the contrast between communication and attention to provide some grounds for the claim that related conceptual distinctions are available in this area.[9] Hall and Whannel stress the close relationship between artist, art and audience in popular culture. They suggest that such culture depends for its popularity on the continuing reaffirmation of known attitudes, values and opinions among the audience. The audience responds by recognizing familiarity. This is in sharp contrast to the traditional claim on behalf of 'high art', that it enables the audience to 'see the world afresh'. In that case the audience responds to new perspectives and unfamiliarity. Hall and Whannel have no doubt that mass art is a corruption of the conventions of popular art, brought about by the mass media's need to be sure of a large audience. Various processes of standardization remove those particular references appealing to specific audience groups which are to be found in popular art. The new art form becomes available to an undifferentiated mass audience. Mass art has to rely primarily on universal emotional reactions. The result is a form of art which is available to everyone but has nothing to say to anyone.

It seems likely that the different types of art distinguished by Hall and Whannel will be the result of different production orientations. 'High art' is believed to be the product of individual creative genius. In W. H. Auden's words 'the interests of a writer and the interests of his readers are never the same and if, on occasion, they happen to coincide, this is a lucky accident'. Such work is often spoken of as something which the artist had to create, regardless of audience and critical reaction. It is even doubtful whether this type of individual artist can be said to be working for himself in a complementary role as audience. Although it may be possible to develop such an orientation in the newer media the closest approach to it commonly found seems to be to put oneself and/or one's immediate colleagues into the role of audience. Colleagues are readily available and moreover they share many of the perspectives and assumptions which are held in common within the media culture. On occasions *The Nature of Prejudice* production team worked for themselves as their own audience. An example was the inclusion of the film clip showing riotous fans after one of the 'prejudiced' interviewees had suggested that Englishmen were traditionally reserved and restrained. It was open to the audience to recognize the intentions behind this insert and to react in the same way. But the important feature of the audience relationship to this type of production orientation is that it depends on coincidence between the interests of the producers and the audience.

This point may be illustrated by the results of another case study carried out on two programmes, in a series of topical, satirical, entertainment programmes produced by Danish Radio for a youth audience.[10] These programmes, called *Peppermill*, were produced by a group of young journalists and television personnel. Production of each programme took place within a week and was centred on a series of production meetings. In these meetings the producers used each other as a sounding board for their ideas and to test reaction to the completed material. The producers made little reference to the audience except to assume that they would respond in the same way as themselves. Audience research carried out as part of the study suggested that the programmes were not strikingly popular. Young people criticized the programmes mainly on the grounds that they could not understand them, that they were too boring or that they dealt at too great a length with serious political subjects. But within the general *Peppermill* audience there was a small group of 'devotees' who followed the series regularly on television and radio. These devotees liked the programmes and generally recognized the production intentions which lay behind them. Only crude socio-economic indices were available from the surveys but the minority group of devotees appeared to be more like the production team than the rest of the target youth audience. They were older, more intelligent, and among the girls, more likely to be middle class. They tended to live in or around Copenhagen, the metropolitan centre, and they appeared to share, however loosely, the production team's political sympathies. The result was a form of minority, 'special public' communication within the setting of a mass medium.

No doubt one of the skills in production work for a mass medium is the ability to empathize with audience groups of which one is not a member. Some producers seem to have favourite target audience groups. They use their imagined reaction as a yardstick against which to judge a production. Such producers may hit on a programme that strikes a chord for a large audience group and it becomes in Hall and Whannel's terms – popular culture. There is also the chance that they will miss their audience and end up in the situation of the *Peppermill* producers, working only for a minority of 'devotees'. Comparable conclusions could be drawn from the world of newspaper publishing where some publishers, and to a lesser extent editors, have succeeded in creating papers with definite identities which have appealed to large but distinctive audiences. Others have developed papers with distinct identities which have failed to find a large market, while others have sought to increase audience size and advertising revenue by abandoning rather than creating such identities.

But the reference to audience size and advertising revenue suggests that this production orientation is likely to be under continual pressure. It is inherently uncertain. Such pressure shows itself in, for example, the repetition of standardized genres, the avoidance of material which might provoke offence and generally in the attempt to be all things to all men. At the production level, it is reflected in a third orientation towards audience attention. The disparity between high art and standardized genres has generally been explained in terms of conflict between artistic creativity and the commercial and administrative concerns of large-scale media organizations.

So far in this chapter, discussion has been confined to the production level within the medium. Such concentration is justified by the relative autonomy which appears to be enjoyed by those working at this level in British television. Nevertheless, it is important not to lose sight of the over-arching commercial and organizational structures within which the production teams operate. These structures, just as much as the production personnel within them, can be seen as mediating between society as source and society as audience.

The society as source influences the media organizations by setting the conditions for their survival and growth. Clearly some groups in society are in a better position to influence these conditions than others. In Britain there have also been variations in the requirements which the two broadcasting systems have been expected to meet. This study was carried out within commercial television, but it is useful to consider briefly some of the changes which have occurred in the situation of the BBC. The institutional structure of the BBC was explicitly designed to provide some insulation between communication and commercialism. Throughout the period during which the BBC had a monopoly in broadcasting it was able to play a considerable part in defining its own role. This established independence for the BBC from the immediate demands of the mass audience. Instead, the BBC had support from various custodians of the cultural heritage. Ironically, the most recent activities of members of this group, in the form of the Campaign for Better Broadcasting, have been directed against the BBC, specifically against changes in BBC Radio. The introduction of commercial television gave fuller expression to the mass characteristics of the television medium and changed the situation in which the BBC operated. To safeguard its case for future increases in the licence fee, it had to set about competing for the audience as a mass. A further irony is that the BBC has since been blamed for succeeding in this endeavour, often by the same people who supported, or who now claim to have supported, its previous role as cultural custodian. Some have even gone so far as to stand the case against the BBC as a monopoly on its head, claiming that there is now no difference between the two popular television channels so that the continued existence of the BBC as a separate institution cannot be justified. Such an argument begs a variety of questions, not least whether the two channels are really so similar. The argument has mainly been advanced for political purposes, but even so it provides an apposite illustration of a shift in the conditions under which one television organization has operated.

Another example, drawn from the present study itself, shows how the organizational structure of ITV may on occasions temper the dictates of commercialism. At the time *The Nature of Prejudice* was in production the prospect of the reallocation of contracts made documentary production especially advantageous to the companies as a means of impressing the Authority. Both British television systems show how variations in organization structure can modify the simple equation between mass audience and mass medium. The ability to judge consumer demand is one, but only one way of ensuring the survival and growth of the television organizations. It is also necessary to bear in mind the conditions set by other constituents.

The traditional dispute between creative personnel and administrators in the media can be seen as a special case of the problem of reconciling professional authority and consumer demand. Professional expertise may suggest a course of action which would not be that preferred by the customer. In some professions, notably medicine, professional expertise is presumed to be sovereign, in other fields it may still be accepted that the customer is 'always right'. An additional problem in the case of the mass media is that communicators and administrators have to make guesses about audiences' needs and tastes on the basis of inadequate information. Administrators are likely to be guided in the guesses they make by the view they take of the organization's other constituents and their demands. On the other hand the creative personnel are likely to adopt one of the three orientations towards the audience outlined above. Although it is a common answer to problems of media organization to advocate more professionalism, more creative autonomy for the programme producer, a distinction needs to be drawn between professional autonomy in developing standard procedures for dealing with recurrent work tasks, and creative autonomy, which in the high cultural sense would lead to individuation rather than standardization of output. Professionalism may take the form of a concentration on routine procedures for handling problems posed by television production so that the occupational group becomes even more inward looking, as a separate system intervening between source and audience.

The model of the mass communication process, developed in this book, consists of three separate systems, society as source, mass communicators and society as audience. Each of these systems takes from the other what is necessary for its own needs. The mass communicators draw on society for material suitable for their purposes, the audience is left largely on its own to respond to the material put before it. Each system has its own set of interests and its own ways of bringing influence to bear on the others. This model is in direct contrast to those which link the different parts of the communication process directly, conceptualizing it as a process of influence or communication flow. The model can be clarified by substituting the term 'spectator' for the audience. The analogy is with the spectators at, for example, a tennis match. They sit outside the court and watch the game. If mass communication was a process of direct influence or transmittal of meaning the players would turn round and hit their balls into the crowd. This is an over extreme case to argue from the present study. More comparative work is needed before it can be said to have been established. But if communication is defined as the transference of ordered meaning, the paradox suggested by the present study is that mass communication is liable not to be communication at all.

This claim, that the dominant means of communication cannot be used for communication, raises wider issues about the relationship between the media and society which can only be touched on here. First, it is inevitable that if the main focus in

programme production is on audience attention and satisfaction, the main dimension of possible audience reaction will
be emotional response to familiar symbols. McCluhan has
argued that the electronic, visual media are about to change the
whole sensory and cognitive style to which we have become
accustomed through the literary media. The argument suggested
by this book is that a shift towards emotionalism and symbolism is not just a consequence of the different inherent qualities
of the different media. It is a result of the gradual progression
towards media showing more and more mass characteristics in
content and organization. C. Wright Mills had a phrase for it.
In mass society he argued the public have become 'mere media
markets'; a phrase which reflects not simply the spread of commercialism, but also the change in the relationship between
people and society from the nineteenth-century view of a community of publics.[11]

A second issue is that although the professional communicator has gradually emerged as a new-style intellectual in
society, the tendency is for him to be preoccupied with the form
rather than the content of communication. On the other hand
those who are preoccupied with content are not likely to achieve
access to the form. The factors which inhibit the broadcasters'
opportunities to communicate through the media, also ensure
that they will be unlikely to provide society, in Mannheim's
terms, with any 'free floating' intellectual challenge.[12]

Together these two issues contribute to a third which is best
expressed in the familiar question – does the output of the
media necessarily maintain consensus and the status quo? The
first argument about the relationship possible between the
audience and the media seems to support a Marcusian view of
a mass population available for manipulation. However, the
second argument suggests that those working in the media are
not able to exercise sufficient direct control over its output to
engage in such direct manipulation. This does not mean, however, that nothing is said, that no effect is produced, that no
manipulation takes place. What is said is the unplanned product

of following accepted production routines within established organizational systems. As a result it must be expected that what is said will in the main be fundamentally supportive of the socio-economic structure of the society in which those organizations are set.

Nevertheless, the argument that mass communication is not communication is an extreme one, designed not as an absolute assertion but to focus attention on a tendency. This book has been based on one study. Among the variety of programmes on television today there are some which seem to have more communicative meaning, to be less conventionally reflective than others. One of the common sense arguments which appears to contradict the view of the media as system-maintaining is that in most sections of television at least the predominant ethos continues to be liberal-progressive. But such an ethos, and even occasional programmes which seem to be a direct reflection of it, cannot by themselves refute the argument of this book that the more mass the media the more inhibitions are placed on a direct communication process. It may seem paradoxical to argue that the dominant means of communication in society is tending more and more to be controlled and operated by people who have nothing to say, or if they have, cannot use the media to say it. It does suggest, however, that the mass media illustrate the contradictions rather than the conspiracies of capitalist society.

REFERENCES

1. T. McCormack, 'Social Theory and the Mass Media', *Canadian Review of Economics and Political Science*, 27, 1961, pp. 479–489.

2. B. H. Westley and M. S. Maclean, jnr., 'A Conceptual Model for Communication Research', *Journalism Quarterly*, 34, 1957, pp. 31–38.

3. For an elaboration of a similar argument in another case study see J. D. Halloran, P. Elliott and G. Murdock, *Communication and Demonstrations: A Case Study* (Harmondsworth: Penguin) 1970.

4. The programme was *Men against Cancer* made by Associated Rediffusion and networked on ITV in September, 1967. The study of cancer professionals was carried out by Philip Elliott. A study of a sample of the general public was also conducted by Roger L. Brown. Reports are forthcoming.

5. A. Strauss, L. Schatzman, R. Bucher, D. Ehrlich and M. Sabshin, *Psychiatric Ideologies and Institutions* (New York: Free Press) 1964.

6. See J. D. Halloran *et al. op. cit.*, pp. 185–186 for a discussion of this point.

7. *Ibid.*, especially ch. 6.

8. See for example the various recent accounts on 'the making' and 'the selling' of a number of political figures.

9. S. Hall and P. Whannel, *The Popular Arts* (London: Hutchinson) 1964.

10. J. D. Halloran and P. Elliott, *Peberkvaernen* (Copenhagen: Danish Radio) 1970.

11. C. Wright Mills, *The Power Elite* (New York: Oxford University Press) 1959.

12. K. Mannheim, *Ideology and Utopia* (London: Routledge) 1936. Anyone who cherishes a belief that academics can fill such a role, or who suspects that I hold such a belief, should read Alvin Gouldner's, *The Coming Crisis of Western Sociology* (London: Heinemann) 1971.

Appendix A

1 *Types of Content in the Programmes* (percentage of running time).

Type of Content	Programme No.						
	1	2	3	4	5	6	7
Archive film	9·7	0	1·8	15·4	0	0	0
Filmed interview	51·5	22·1	42·5	9·6	22·5	14·4	0
Filmed experiments	3·6	11·7	0	12·0	2·7	0	0
'Vox Pop'	6·1	0	0·5	1·0	0	0	0
Presenter's links	29·1	5·8	27·2	11·9	10·3	7·2	4·8
Studio guests	0	60·4	28·0	50·1	64·5	78·4	92·8
Total	100·0	100·0	100·0	100·0	100·0	100·0	100·0

2 *Summary outlines* (*prepared for this book*)

Programme I illustrated the variety of prejudice, through different definitions, historical examples and contemporary accounts. At the end the question, 'What causes prejudice?' was raised.

Programme II concentrated on the development of prejudice among children as seen by various individuals and as studied by Dr. Pushkin with various social psychological experiments. It ended with a discussion between Dr. Pushkin, another social psychologist Dr. J. Field, and the presenter.

Programme III looked at the relationship between prejudice and membership of a group through individuals' views and experiences and through a concluding discussion with Professor Hilde Himmelweit.

Programme IV examined the process of stereotyping in feature films, in the experiences of distinct social groups and in the experimental work of Professor Henri Tajfel who was also joined in the discussion by Dr. Field.

Programme V took up education and legislation as alternative methods of dealing with prejudice in contemporary society. In the studio, Professor Marie Jahoda discussed education, Anthony Lester, legislation.

Programme VI was an attempt to investigate in the studio the views of three 'prejudiced' individuals, James Mottram who was questioned on race and colour, Lady Dartmouth on young people, sex and pornography, and Peregrine Worsthorne on social élitism.

Programme VII concluded the series with a wide-ranging studio discussion on the phenomenon of prejudice, between Professor Henri Tajfel, Professor A. J. Ayer and Mark Bonham Carter.

Appendix B

Participant observation, more than most methods in social research, seems to attract extreme reactions from critics and enthusiasts. Its advantages lie in the possibility of tackling social process and relationships within the social situation. It is not simply a way of studying individuals but of individuals within society, covering not only beliefs and behaviour but also the characteristic features of the setting as observed and as experienced by the actors. A commonly held middle position in evaluating the method is that it is a legitimate first step in exploratory research which can then be backed up by other techniques. This is reasonable in so far as one of the basic problems in social research is to establish frequency of occurrence and then to relate different frequencies to show the interaction of phenomena.[1] But such a relationship once found requires explanation. The researcher can then draw on established social theory and on his own experience of living within the society to make sense of his findings. It is to be hoped that he will have taken steps to ensure that his experience is not completely divorced from that of his subjects. In this way all social research can be said to depend on the participant observations made by the researcher through his ordinary life experience. But different research techniques should be seen as complementary, differently suited to a variety of research problems, rather than ranged in a hierarchy in which participant observation is relegated to preliminary status.

An alternative approach to the investigation of frequency, which establishes the value of participant observation in its own right, is to delve into a situation rather than abstract from it and from others presumed to be like it. Such delving leads to generalizations of a different type. It draws attention to the patterns of interaction which are likely to develop between men and their physical and socio-cultural environments. Moreover observation is not exclusively 'man centred' but can deal with other socio-cultural phenomena as they impinge upon social action. Such generalizations can be established not only by doing frequency research but by doing more comparative participant observation studies in a variety of settings. In the sense that no research is ever finished, participant observation can be said to be as exploratory as any other method.

Nevertheless the aim of this appendix is not so much to debate the merits of the method in general as to examine some of the problems of applying it to this particular case.[2] Researcher and researched in this study came from much the same social level (though clearly at different stages of individual careers) as evidenced, for example, by the fact that three of the production team and the researcher had all been to Oxford University.* There was no initial problem of socio-cultural distance such as faces the social anthropologist in a tribal society or the sociologist in a slum community. This obviated the need for a lengthy run-up period to sensitize the researcher to a new way of life. The organizational and occupational cultures which were the subject of study were all part of the same socio-cultural system to which research and the researcher belonged. It has been argued that distance is necessary to objectify the situation researched. But while distance may encourage a feeling of objectivity, it is anything but a guarantee that the researcher has completely understood the dynamics of

---

* In this appendix I have mainly adopted a personal style to recount the problems as I saw them, following Whyte's classic example in the appendix to *Street Corner Society*. Where the researcher is mentioned in the third person the reference is to myself, not the television researcher.

the social experience. Distance may also help at a later stage in the making of broad generalizations, but this seems to be more an argument for a comparative approach than for distance *per se*.

Nevertheless, there were a number of problems in fitting into the television production situation. With so few people involved in the core production team there seemed to be a real danger that the intrusion of another would drastically alter the situation. For this reason I adopted the role which Strauss and his colleagues have identified as that of 'passive observer with minimal clarifying interaction'.[3] Possible observer roles vary, according to the range and type of participation in the situation they involve. Each of these has various advantages and disadvantages.

One of the disadvantages of the passive observer role is that it takes some time to win acceptance for it. Once it has won acceptance it provides a secure basis from which to widen the range and scope of interaction. One finds oneself involved in general conversations on one's own terms from which useful data on a wide variety of topics can be gathered. Doc's advice to Whyte has extremely general validity. 'Go easy on that "who", "what", "why", "when", "where" stuff, Bill ... If people accept you, you can just hang around, and you'll learn the answers in the long run without even having to ask the questions.'[4] Getting accepted, however, involves personal difficulties for the researcher as well as for the group. In this case, unwilling to trust my memory, I took notes constantly as the production team was working. Not unnaturally members of the team were continually puzzled and occasionally suspicious about what I was noting. Note-taking was also important personally as it gave me something to do. There are problems in justifying an observer role to oneself, especially in an occupational milieu like that of television with its emphasis on the projection of personal charisma. One such problem was whether to get involved in general discussions within the team, especially during the early planning and researching stages. I tried to avoid this, initially adopting a rule of not speaking until spoken to and then saying as little as possible consistent with not appearing rude or completely vacant. Again, however, it was not surprising to find some people suspicious of an apparently silent presence (although I did use words to explain what I was doing!). Acceptance is only a matter of time, however, helped by sharing common experiences.

These difficulties were really important only with people briefly and peripherally involved in the production process with whom there was little time to establish rapport and little extended interaction to observe. In this study I considered the idea of carrying out specific interviews with interviewees, studio guests and more peripheral production personnel. I rejected this partly because I felt it would change the focus of the research by bringing in additional interesting but peripheral questions and also because I did not want to impose a structure at that stage on the way the data emerged from the process. Such interviews could well be a valuable addition on another occasion, always providing they could be carried out without interfering with production work.

In my note-taking I tried to record both the substance of discussion and behaviour and the patterns of interaction and relationships involved in it. I adopted a strategy, tenable as a basic position in the philosophy of social science, that nothing was irrelevant. There was usually only time to cover the situation partially so I concentrated on the substance, remaining conscious of the interaction pattern in order to understand the social meaning of the situation, even though it could not be rigorously analysed. My initial plan to make sense of the material was to order it around the different individuals involved, to study the role which each played in the process. To this end I transferred each day's notes onto sheets summarizing who had done what with whom. At the same time propositions began to emerge concentrating on the process and its social setting more than on the individuals involved and in the course of research and analysis this perspective took over. Who decides what became much less important than trying to unravel the characteristic features of the production process in its social setting.

Such a view was already contained in the theoretical formulation of the project prepared before the research started. Once in the field the practical problems of following what was going on, deciding what to record when and managing my own interaction in the situation became so engrossing that initial theory appeared to have little relevance. Then came the stage, known in the literature as 'going native', in which I began to recognize beliefs and actions so clearly that it was hard to imagine how they could be different. The data acquired a shape based in a descriptive sense on the way the process appeared. The initial write up of this study ran to well over 200,000 words and played a crucial part in the analysis process. I felt I had to put as much as possible on paper, both to justify the data to myself and to others, and because I could not distance myself from it while it was only partially analysed but all interrelated in my mind. Working from the initial write-up focused the process which had been going on throughout the research, of formulating ideas and then checking them against the data. The second version and the third (this book) became progressively less descriptive, sharpening up the analysis and cutting down the length. I am very conscious of the twin dangers, however, of allowing the analysis to take leave of the data and of not presenting the full evidence in a digestible form. The important test to apply to the analysis of participant observation data seems to me not to be simply how many other cases is this likely to be true for – a question which cannot be answered within the terms of the method; but how plausible is the posited relationship between belief, behaviour and situation in the light of possible alternative explanations? Obviously these two criteria are not entirely separate, but the point can perhaps be summarized by saying that the aim in case study research is to spell out the mechanisms of social behaviour and relationship accounting for their occurrence in their social setting. Finding the reason for a phenomenon is not something which comes later but is an integral part of observation on which later generalization rests.

As successive written versions of this study have become more focused, less descriptive, they have also lost many personal references to the individuals involved. The convention of anonymity has been followed even though such a small group in such a visible setting will inevitably be recognized by many in the medium and outside. Nevertheless, observing the convention serves to underline the point that although this is a study of individuals it is about structure and process. A copy of the first write-up was seen by those centrally involved in the production. This was particularly useful as a check on fact and interpretation and also on individual sensitivities, enabling me to leave out some personal references, marginal to the study. It is important to emphasize, however, that this did not involve any form of censorship. The ethical problems implicit in publishing field work loom particularly large in a case such as this when those researched, their colleagues and friends may be expected to read the published work.[5] On the other hand this fact also provides a challenging opportunity to involve those outside, as well as those inside, the academic community in the perspectives and problems of social science.

1. On this point see especially H. Blumer, 'Sociological Analysis and the "Variable"', in J. G. Manis and B. N. Meltzer (eds.), *Symbolic Interaction* (Boston: Allyn and Bacon) 1967.

2. Readers who wish to pursue this topic should consult A. Cicourel, *Method and Measurement in Social Science* (London: Collier-Macmillan) 1964; B. Glaser and A. Strauss, *The Discovery of Grounded Theory* (London: Weidenfeld and Nicolson) 1967; A. Strauss *et al.*, *Psychiatric Ideologies and Institutions* (New York: Free Press) 1964; G. J. McCall and J. L. Simmons, *Issues in Participant Observation* (London: Addison Wesley) 1969; S. T. Bruyn, *The Human Perspective in Sociology: The Methodology of Participant Observation* (Englewood Cliff, N.J.: Prentice Hall) 1966.

3. A. Strauss *et al.* (1964).

4. W. F. Whyte, *Street Corner Society* (London: University of Chicago Press) 2nd edn. 1965, p. 303.

5. For a useful discussion see Howard S. Becker, 'Problems in the Publication of Field Studies' in G. J. McCall and J. L. Simmons, *op. cit.*

Index